'Annual reports are in a five
That's the amount of time, according to
statistics, that the average reader will
give the book before tossing it aside.'
Communications World

How to produce
inspiring annual reports

CONTENTS

Introduction

> If we can't present this work compellingly, with pace and passion that will inspire action, then we are doing something terribly wrong.

The inspiration business

Almost by definition, anything written about the exploits and achievements of the voluntary sector should be inspirational. More than any other business area, the enterprises we work for – charities, arts organisations, educational, campaigning and similar groups – have access to stories and images capable of inspiring and motivating people on a massive scale.

Voluntary organisations routinely deal with life and death issues. They can tell the extraordinary stories of ordinary people aspiring to the highest of ideals in education, the arts, in campaigning for social change, to end hunger, to save our environment, eradicate killer diseases, relieve the plight of refugees, house the homeless and generally make the world a better place. If we can't present this work compellingly, with pace and passion that will inspire action, then we are doing something terribly wrong.

Annual reports, why bother?

Much has changed since this book's predecessor, *Charity Annual Reports*, first challenged voluntary and campaigning organisations to take a more entrepreneurial view of how they communicate. In 1987, Ken Burnett wrote: 'Many charities are spending a great deal to print and send out publications that will never be read. In an area where everyone purports to be concerned about sensible use of resources, this is conspicuous waste.' In the 1980s, notions of supposed economy and a general dearth of communication skills led many voluntary organisations to send through the letterboxes of Britain dull, ill-thought-out and under-designed communications that had little chance of ever really reaching their readers. The worst offender was usually the annual report. Thankfully, those days are now past.

Now everyone accepts that charities and similar organisations must communicate effectively with a variety of important audiences. Everyone knows too that they have to do so in an increasingly noisy and competitive environment. In recent years many voluntary organisations have invested substantial sums in writing, design and photography for printed and electronic communication. And in the last decade computer-assisted design has arrived on everyone's desktop. So now voluntary organisations clearly have both the motivation and the means to produce excellent, inspirational communications.

Yet few do. For although they generally look better and there are more of them, most free publications still fail to really capture their intended readers. Many good-looking, expensively designed publications *still* don't have a focus and have neither identified their key messages nor built up a clear picture of their typical reader, or an understanding of their readers' lives. Many organisations still write for themselves and assume too much knowledge and interest on the part of the reader. They don't use design that helps readers or words that draw them into the organisation and its achievements.

It's not a question of how big you are or how much you spend. Despite investing large sums and lots of effort to make their publications *look* good, many voluntary organisations still don't get good value for money and achieve little impact. In contrast, many smaller organisations with tiny budgets achieve much greater impact because they have invested their time and effort in understanding their readers, so have produced simple but effective communications, tailor-made for the interests of their individual audience.

With a growing emphasis on the need to communicate and the current proliferation of new, particularly electronic, media, voluntary organisations seem set to spend even more on communication in the future. Whether they will continue to get mediocre returns on this investment remains to be seen.

Aspire to inspire
In this book we hope to show you why, in the future, success for any organisation will increasingly depend on its ability to produce effective, involving, *relevant* communications that stand out from the herd. We also hope to show why, if they are to be effective and involving, above all communications must inspire.

There's so much competition for your readers' attention these days that if you wish to be read you really had better aspire to inspire. If you need to motivate action, to raise funds, or get bums out of armchairs for special events you'll just have to be inspirational. If you wish to avoid wasting whatever sums your employers (ie your supporters) invest on communications sent uninvited into the congested, noisy and over-hyped world where your busy readers live, you absolutely must send something inspirational. If you yearn to stand out from your competitors in this era of soundbites and the 15-second attention span then being inspirational isn't optional, it's mandatory.

▲ Fifteen years and a dramatic improvement in visual presentation separate these two front covers from Imperial Cancer Research Fund. Gloomy, uninspiring photographs have been replaced by a lively, friendly cover which puts people at the heart ▼ of the organisation's work.

Eight reasons for producing a good annual report

1 A good annual report explains your organisation to the outside world. It tells the story of your aims, achievements, commitment and style of working.

2 A good annual report reports back to donors and others. A bad one can destroy a donor's confidence.

3 A good annual report is your sales brochure to new and old customers. A bad one discourages potential supporters.

4 A good annual report encourages staff and volunteers, giving them pride in their employer and work.

5 A good annual report motivates and attracts quality applicants, whereas a bad one will put people off.

6 A good annual report gives a clear picture of sound stewardship, showing good use of your supporters' money.

7 A good annual report can directly solicit involvement and raise money.

8 A good annual report reinforces public trust and gives credibility to the organisation and the voluntary sector as a whole. A bad one can destroy credibility for all voluntary organisations.

There's a fair amount of truth in the old publishing cliché that says producing publications is ten per cent inspiration and 90 per cent perspiration. But for producers of free publications it could be dangerously misleading.

It'll come as no surprise to anyone that producing publications involves lots of hard slog, and the potentially high costs of production coupled with the manifold risks of failure can easily cause even the bravest to perspire. So perspiration there is aplenty in publications production. But if inspiration is just one-tenth of what adds up to success then it should be recognised from the start that this minority component is fundamentally important. It's the Holy Grail. It's where modern-day communications, particularly in the not-for-profit sector, either succeed or fail.

And most free communications do fail. Even among those publications that succeed in getting past the first major hurdle (will intended readers even open the envelope, let alone start to read and digest the contents?) many won't get much further, perhaps because organisations have structured their message inappropriately, failed to understand their readers, have concentrated on themselves rather than their cause, or forgotten to take account of where they fit in their readers' lives ... More likely they will fail to encourage more than a superficial further reading simply because they are dull. Even a cursory analysis of a selection of free publications from Britain's leading voluntary organisations will confirm that this genus of communication suffers from a propensity to be dull. Of those that are not dull, many are simply not working as hard as they might. And for today's busy reader, this is just not good enough. So the majority of free publications end before they've really started, becoming just more waste paper.

This may seem depressing but really it's great news for you. If inspiring others is the part where most free communications fail, for you it's a golden opportunity. It's where you and your organisation have the best chance of getting just a little bit ahead of all the other causes and issues that clamour daily for the attention of your readers.

This book shows you how to do it.

© Philip Meech

Before a word is written or a
picture chosen you have to get
your thinking right. What role
or roles do you want your
annual report to fulfil? How
does your annual report fit in
to your overall strategy? Who
do you want to reach, and why?
What are the messages you
want to convey? What are the
strategic points you wish to
make? And what kind of
response do you aim to inspire?

The Teachers' Benevolent Fund used its annual report 1998/99
to launch its new name, TBF: the teacher support network, and
position itself as a charity supporting teachers in their daily lives.

5

1 Getting the thinking right

Who could you be talking to with your annual report?

- Your current supporters
- Trusts and foundations
- Corporate partners
- Central and local government
- Other opinion formers
- Local authority funders/ contract partners
- The general enquirer
- Potential new supporters
- Potential legators
- Your board of trustees
- Solicitors and other advisers
- Your staff
- Volunteers
- The media
- Potential new recruits
- Beneficiaries
- Your suppliers

Making the most of your key communications

You may picture your target businesswoman elbowing aside all the rest of her day's mail in favour of your clearly flagged envelope, postponing a waiting stack of e-mails to avidly consume your carefully crafted *œuvre*. Or, when your annual report arrives unheralded through the letterbox you may imagine a family crowding round eager for a look, or waiting patiently in turn until the others are finished.

Scenes like these rarely happen.

Understand your readers

The truth is we live in a noisy world, where hundreds of different interests compete for our readers' attention. Nobody *has* to read your annual report, nor any of your other free publications. It's unlikely to be a high priority with most of your readers. So it's up to you to do everything you can to make your communications accessible and irresistible.

To do that you have first to identify, then really understand, your readers. Then you have to tell them, in a way they will like and have time for, the most involving story you have, illustrating it with your most appealing photographs and informative charts and diagrams. But to be fully accessible you also have to pitch it right, so it says the right things to the right people in the right way; so it arrives at the right time in packaging that begs to be opened; so it contains just the right calls to action and an easy response device. Finally it has to be followed up properly so lessons learned this year can be applied to improve next year's publication.

More than this, your annual report has to be researched properly in advance and planned correctly so its content fits in with your organisation's overall communications strategy. You have to ensure that its structure, contents and principal messages all reinforce each of the concepts you want your main audiences not just to appreciate but to thoroughly understand and sign up to. It has to reinforce your brand image generally and strengthen your standing with certain key groups. It has to be capable of moving people from where they are to where you want them to be. It has to give your readers what you want them to have, and give them an easy way to do what you want them to do.

To fully appreciate its importance, just consider its potential influence with your key audiences (see panel left).

Plan and prepare carefully

And all this applies equally whether you have a staff of thousands or are on your own, the proverbial one-man or one-woman band. Indeed, if you represent a small organisation this may well be even more important for you, as chances are you won't have many other media to support your annual report, so it will have to do all these important jobs on its own.

It probably goes without saying that any publication that does such a vital job for your organisation deserves careful planning and preparation, and if it is to do its job properly it's unlikely to be easy or cheap to produce. But it's worth reminding ourselves that just because it's important to us, that doesn't mean all our intended readers will view it with equal importance.

And unless we are very clever, they may not see it as important at all.

Living with the waste-paper basket

'Annual reports are in a five-minute race. That's the amount of time, according to statistics, that the average reader will give the book before tossing it aside.' So said the magazine *Communication World*. In the course of researching this book we found people give even less time – maybe three minutes if you're lucky. So perhaps the secret of success is to make those few minutes really count.

It does no harm to have the image of the waste-paper basket firmly fixed in your mind if not actually pictured, icon-like, on the wall in front of you as a sobering reminder to would-be authors and publishers of the fate that awaits most free media.

But don't be put off if you only have a few minutes of your reader's attention. In those brief moments, your dramatic cover image can make a powerful impact, your moving photographs can leave a lasting memory, your snappy captions can fix a lingering impression and your punchy headlines and call-outs can get the essence of your main messages across even if reading the text is reserved for later – or never happens.

Be not dismayed. These few moments may be all that many of your most valuable supporters will need to be reassured that all is well with their favourite cause, that it is proceeding as they would wish, is continuing to punch above its weight and is as committed as ever to being accountable to its donors.

Meet your reader

'The annual report is important for people like me because it represents the organisation as a whole, rather than just the project we may be being asked to support. It describes the environment in which that project exists.

'The annual report is a powerful tool to reinforce or undermine the messages and values the charity is putting forward. There needs to be consistency – if there isn't, it can influence how you view a grant application.

'It also needs to give an understanding of the finances of an organisation. If the annual report doesn't meet SORP guidelines, it won't go down too well. We don't mind receiving a summary, but send us the full accounts as well.

'However, staff and trustees are not robots! Yes, some trusts are very tight on their criteria and use a scoring system to determine who to award money to. But there are many others where it would be crazy to think that personal reactions to a charity's work and the way the charity talks about it can be ignored.'

David Carrington, Chief Executive, PPP Healthcare Medical Trust.

Most voluntary organisations appeared in no rush to respond to a request for their annual report. Average response time was more than two weeks, with many taking a leisurely four weeks or more to get their standard responses in the post.

How charities produce and use publications

Good practice in terms of how publications are produced and subsequently used is really common sense. If asked, most readers of this book would expect any reasonably competent voluntary sector communicator to have set up a sensibly structured internal editorial and production function. This, most readers might again expect, would be tasked not to produce publications in a vacuum but to monitor and evaluate its output and ensure that any requests, queries or feedback from readers would be appropriately dealt with, promptly and efficiently.

So one might expect. The problem is that practice frequently differs from intentions, and it's on practice that our audiences judge us.

Please don't bother us

To establish just how good or otherwise current communications practice is among not-for-profit organisations, Burnett Associates recently commissioned two studies into how charities produce and use their publications*. The research involved two types of 'mystery shopping' test among organisations selected at random from the nation's top charities. The first asked general questions, the second was specific to annual reports. In addition, 15 leading charities completed a detailed questionnaire covering aspects of their publications' functions and structure.

The lessons learned were many and shortage of space permits only the briefest summary here (anyone wishing for more details can contact the authors – see inside front cover). But the conclusions were quite damning.

The quality of response and importance given to publications were inconsistent, as might be expected. Few charities have communications strategies of any kind, or have any strategic overview of their publications' functions. Guidelines on how to deal with enquiries are rare and as a result the general enquirer may be politely treated but is unlikely to be either quickly or effectively answered. Guidance on how to access information in publications, or even what publications exist, is also rare. The person answering phones or letters is rarely linked to the publications function. Perhaps these are among the reasons why voluntary organisations fare so badly at customer service.

*How readers read, A research study © 1997 Burnett Associates Limited

Did Monica write to you?

Continuing our undercover surveillance, in November 1999 a would-be donor (our plant) Mrs Monica Blakeley wrote to 50 medium and large not-for-profits (see right) requesting a copy of their annual report. A more promising enquiry would be hard to imagine.

Mrs B's postbag over the next six to eight weeks was mixed, to say the least. All but six recipients of her letter responded, a failure rate above ten per cent. As asked, most sent their annual report often accompanied by a bewildering array of additional enclosures.

Most appeared in no rush. Average response time was over two weeks, with many taking a leisurely four weeks or more to get their standard responses in the post.

What did she get back?

Most notable shortcomings in the reports themselves were organisational obsession (just writing for themselves) and drabness. Change the name of the organisation and many reports could be from just about anyone. Some seemed stuck in a time warp, using design that would have been dull even in the 1950s.

But others were a treat. The Prince's Trust sent a brilliant annual report in the format of a calendar, but curiously the year covered was 1996/97. A few reports (Shelter, NCH Action For Children) excelled in their reports because of the way they used words and pictures to tell a powerful story. Two reports stood out from the rest because of their striking outer envelopes (all the others followed drab convention). Plan International's envelope had been cunningly designed to look like an aerogram letter. It cried out 'open me first!' The other was from Barnardo's, who cleverly started their story on the outer envelope, which acted as a trailer for the contents.

Fewer than one in five bothered to include a personalised covering letter to our Monica. Many omitted even a compliment slip. Only the Guildhall School of Music directly referred in its covering letter to its urgent need for financial support. The British Library also gave Monica some idea of the difference her support could make. Staggeringly, one report was ushered in not by a friendly letter but by an off-putting despatch note which threatened that an invoice would follow.

> Dear Sir or Madam,
>
> I am currently reviewing my regular donations to a small number of charities. Please would you be kind enough to send me an up-to-date copy of your charity annual report? It would also be helpful if you could let me have an issue of any newsletter, magazine or journal that you produce, and anything else you feel may help me.
>
> I look forward to hearing from you.
>
> Yours truly,
>
> Monica Blakeley (Mrs)

▲ 'Our Monica' sent this letter to 50 charities. She expresses an interest in their work and is obviously in the business of giving money away. Yet fewer than one charity in five bothered to send Monica a personal reply.

▲ Open me first! When the first pile of charity packages landed on Monica's doorstep, this one from Plan International, in an airmail envelope, immediately stood out from the crowd.

Many of the accompanying enclosures were quite extraordinary – one charity included a publication on preparing to have a baby. Several recipients seemed to use Monica's request as an opportunity to unload a variety of unwanted materials. We picture a grateful postie heaving a sigh of relief at the end of the test, as he will no longer have to haul charities' responses up to Monica's front door …

But what would our Mrs B make of all this? Well, she'd probably conclude some are getting it right, but they're the minority. As a potential donor, few will have impressed her with their speedy, personal, appropriate response. Those that did were usually, though not always, let down by drab, uninspired and poorly chosen communications. Mrs Blakeley could hardly be blamed for concluding that not-for-profit communicators are not generally very good at what they do, or are very good at wasting money on irrelevant literature. Either that or they're not really interested in the likes of her.

So, it appears, there is plenty of scope for the ambitious communicator who wants to get ahead of the field.

▶ There's some lovely material here, but, with 17 items and no covering letter to point the reader to what might interest her, where does Monica begin?

▶ Which of these covering letters, fronting a range of charity publications, do you think would make the best impression on Monica? Which would make her feel valued, needed, appreciated – a human being with a role to play rather than a cog in a machine?

The Guildhall School of Music (centre) is a cracking example of a hard-working letter. It sets out a specific need Monica might like to help with, emphasises the School's track record in turning out excellent actors and musicians, and invites Monica to come and see the School for herself.

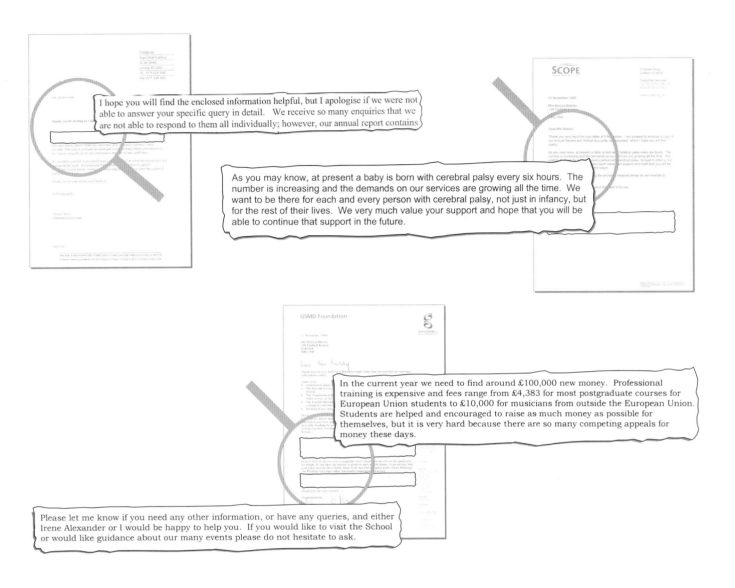

I hope you will find the enclosed information helpful, but I apologise if we were not able to answer your specific query in detail. We receive so many enquiries that we are not able to respond to them all individually; however, our annual report contains

As you may know, at present a baby is born with cerebral palsy every six hours. The number is increasing and the demands on our services are growing all the time. We want to be there for each and every person with cerebral palsy, not just in infancy, but for the rest of their lives. We very much value your support and hope that you will be able to continue that support in the future.

In the current year we need to find around £100,000 new money. Professional training is expensive and fees range from £4,383 for most postgraduate courses for European Union students to £10,000 for musicians from outside the European Union. Students are helped and encouraged to raise as much money as possible for themselves, but it is very hard because there are so many competing appeals for money these days.

Please let me know if you need any other information, or have any queries, and either Irene Alexander or I would be happy to help you. If you would like to visit the School or would like guidance about our many events please do not hesitate to ask.

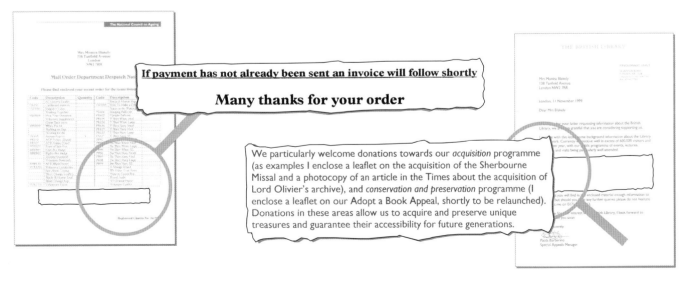

If payment has not already been sent an invoice will follow shortly

Many thanks for your order

We particularly welcome donations towards our *acquisition* programme (as examples I enclose a leaflet on the acquisition of the Sherbourne Missal and a photocopy of an article in the Times about the acquisition of Lord Olivier's archive), and *conservation and preservation* programme (I enclose a leaflet on our Adopt a Book Appeal, shortly to be relaunched). Donations in these areas allow us to acquire and preserve unique treasures and guarantee their accessibility for future generations.

Public confidence monitor

How the British public rates its confidence in its national institutions.

- The Army — 74%
- The Post Office — 69%
- The Police — 58%
- Banks — 46%
- The National Health Service — 40%
- Charities — 33%
- The Church — 25%
- The Government — 11%
- The Media — 7%

Planning for Social Change, The Henley Centre, 1998.

◯ If you listen to your readers in the right way they will tell you not only how your pages should look and what they should say, but how you should approach almost every other aspect of what goes into your annual report.

The changing audience

The only constant these days is change. Everything seems to be forever changing, and not always as we'd like. Communicators in not-for-profit organisations need to anticipate and keep ahead of change, because our audiences too are changing.

Social change appears to be gathering pace. We are not like our parents. Our children may be even less like us. People in the developed world are living longer, are far more widely travelled and have much greater choice in the kind of lives they might lead. Women choose to work, couples decide to be parents later or not at all, people have more assets and disposable cash than ever and less genuinely free time in which to enjoy them. All these changes affect the way your readers judge and consume information.

Today's reader is more likely to be under pressure not just from a busy lifestyle, but also from a seeming explosion of competitive messages intruding into everyday life. There's a new cynicism around (see left) that tells us today's supporter is less likely to take charities at face value and more likely to ask probing, perceptive questions that demand effective answers.

And there are new audiences, each with very different needs, which many not-for-profit organisations need to understand if they are to reach them – local authority purchasers whose business you want to tender for; Government, whose ear you want to bend and whose grants you want to secure; companies whose marketing and grant-giving operations you want to woo.

Not so long ago, many people in voluntary organisations persisted in the belief that their annual report would be read by people just like them. So they wrote for themselves and communicated with no one but themselves. This resulted in dull publications featuring impenetrable messages from endless officials – slabs of grey text enlivened only by a head and shoulders photo of the culprit, in which he or she droned on about departmental achievements in a style even the writer's mother would find uninviting. The phenomenon still exists, but is increasingly rare.

Voluntary organisations of just a few years ago did little to listen to their readers. Now research is very much in vogue and its revelations are transforming the way we communicate.

The importance of research

'Before you can expect your readers to understand you, you must first understand them.' So said David Ogilvy in his book *Confessions of an advertising man*. It's an undeniable truth, but one that still eludes many voluntary organisations.

Some scepticism, as far as research is concerned, is a healthy thing. We know our audiences' views and opinions are changing all the time. Like a photograph of a dancer, research presents a frozen picture of something that is always moving, so the picture, while accurate, shows only part of the truth and then sometimes in a quite misleading light. Even so, little pieces of knowledge can be gold dust and are infinitely better than ignorance.

Charities under-invest in research. As a result they don't understand their products, markets or opportunities nearly well enough, so when they try to communicate their messages to busy audiences success is predictably limited. No sensible commercial organisation would commit a similar false economy.

How to do reader research

Free research. The best research, if perhaps the least orthodox and most unstructured, is to regularly meet your readers face to face and listen to what they say. It takes time and commitment, but nothing beats it for helping you to see your organisation and its communications through your readers' eyes. All other research will seem costly but can be a worthwhile investment.

Telephone interviews are increasingly common, although many consider the telephone to be unduly intrusive. Whether you conduct them yourself or via a specialist agency, make sure your supporters are treated courteously and can decline involvement if they are in the least uncomfortable.

Focus groups are small numbers of randomly selected donors who meet with researchers to answer questions. Expensive, but very informative.

Postal questionnaires. The cheapest and most common method. Results may not be representative as only the more motivated or compulsive form fillers will reply. But a carefully analysed postal questionnaire can unearth a wealth of information. You can ask closed questions for easy comparison or open-ended questions for general impressions. Or, ideally, a mix of both.

What you should know about your readers

- All the demographics: address and phone number, age, sex, children, where they live, what jobs they do, financial status (if possible).

- What are their interests, and how much time do they spend on them?

- What is the most important thing in their lives?

- What other publications do they read and what other charities do they support?

- When would they prefer to hear from you? What would they like to hear about?

- What has their previous relationship with, and behaviour towards, your organisation been like?

- What relationships do they have with similar organisations?

- Do they support your **organisation** or your **cause**?

- What do they respond to and what turns them off?

- What are their views on subjects and interests specific to your organisation?

- How much time do they have?

1 Getting the thinking right

How readers read – the lessons from research

All people are different. So any publication attempting to address a diverse audience has to generalise and make compromises to appeal to the largest possible readership. Nevertheless generations of publishers have amassed a wealth of understanding of what readers want or will accept, and you should seek wherever possible to tap into this. Recent research has given communicators a treasure trove of information on their readers' reading habits and preferences. Even voluntary organisations are beginning to address the need for better understanding of their readers' special needs and interests. The route to this is through research.

But that doesn't mean voluntary organisations have no option but to invest huge sums in research themselves. A vast body of information already exists on how people approach the printed page, from what is most likely to catch their eye to the typical length of their attention span. Academic studies can tell you about the importance of reading gravity (in most Western cultures people read from top left to bottom right) and how they scan-read (apparently in visual sweeps from top right of a spread to bottom right, which stop when the eye lands on a visual hook or 'display item' placed on the page – either deliberately or accidentally).

Summarising the body of science that can be found on readability is beyond the scope of this book but readers would be well advised to familiarise themselves with the work of

Lorem ipsum dolor sit eiusmod tempor incidu enim ad minim veniam oris nisi ut aliquip ex dolor in reprehendert i dolore eu fugiat nulla p praesent luptatum dele non provident, simil to laborum et dolor fuga. liber tempor cum nobis maxim placeat facer p repellend. Temporibu necessit atib saepe even earud reruam hist enta asperiore repellat. Han eam non possing accol tum etia ergat. Nos am cum conscient to facto neque pecun modut est cupiditat, quas nulla p coercend magist and et

let, consectetur adipsci it labore et dolore mag uis nostrud exercitatic commodo consequat. voluptate velit esse mo atur. At vero eos et ao aigue duos dolor et m or sunt in culpa qui c aarumd dereund facilis igend optio comgue nil im omnis voluptas as utem quinusd at aur c ut er repudiand sint et / sapiente delecatus au go cum tene sententiai iodare nost ros quos t et nebevol, olestias ao im poen legum odioqu que nonor imper ned li I om umdant. Improb decendesse videantur.

bene sanos ad iustitiam fact est cond qui neg fa opes vel fortunag vel ii benevolent sib concilia

tuent tamet eum locum Lorem ipsum dolor sit eiusmod tempor incidu enim ad minim veniam oris nisi ut aliquip ex dolor in reprehendert i dolore eu fugiat nulla p praesent luptatum dele

equitated fidem. Nequ : efficerd possit duo co n liberalitat magis cor et, aptissim est ad qui peccand quaert en imi utend inanc sunt is pa usque in insupinaria d iniur. Itaque ne iustiti cunditat vel pluify. Na et luptat pleniore effic d improbitate putamu e rtiuneren guarent ei o loco visetur quibusir que facil, ut mihi detu let, consectetur adipsc it labore et dolore mag uis nostrud exercitati voluptate velit esse mo iatur. At vero eos et ac aigue duos dolor et m

Professor Siegfried Vögele of the Institute of Direct Marketing in Munich, and Colin Wheildon of New South Wales. Luckily all you need to know about these two can be found in Colin Wheildon's brilliant book *Type and Layout*, which is appropriately subtitled *How typography and design can get your message across – or get in the way*. It is amazing to see how persistently its lessons are ignored by professional communicators, and how they lose their readers in droves as a result.

Recent reader research specifically on charity publications also has many useful, practical lessons for not-for-profit communicators (see opposite). Sadly, as a glance at any selection of charity publications will tell you, not all are applied. There is perhaps only one category of not-for-profit communicators harder to understand than those who undertake research then fail to act on its results. It is those who don't see the value in research at all.

Readers scan pages in sweeps starting top right. With minimal display items, the reader's eyes scan only a short distance into the page. More display points give the eyes more fixes and increase the likelihood of the reader going back to digest the message.

Meet your reader

'I'm sure our volunteers read everything we send them, as they're really into what we do.'
   Publications manager, charity.

'I don't really read what they send me.'
   One of the volunteers the above charity suggested we interview.

For obvious reasons we've kept the above quotes anonymous, but they show rather clearly the gap that can exist between how we view our readers and how they view us.

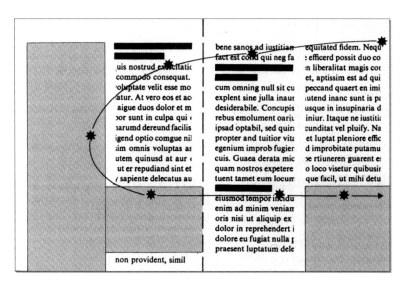

From *Type and Layout* by Colin Wheildon (see Essential reading, page 94).

As with all innovations it can make sense to let others do the pioneering so you can learn from their experiences. You could begin by checking out the sites shown in this section.

▲ Simple, brief, bold and very user-friendly, the Refugee Council's site reflects the organisation's personality. **www.refugeecouncil.org.uk**

The changing media environment

Media isn't what it used to be. In the last decade a new phrase – ambient media – entered our vocabulary. This is jargon for a variety of obscure ways of communicating with the unsuspecting public that until recently were undreamed of even by the most pushy advertising types. 'Ambient' includes such message-carriers as parking meters, petrol pump handles, taxi sides and the lids of take-away curry containers. Even fresh fruit at Tesco isn't immune. If so inclined you can now print your (admittedly rather brief) message on tiny peel-off labels for individual affixing on apples, oranges and similar fare.

These innovations may seem to have little relevance to the not-for-profit communicator, but other recent inventions do and may soon revolutionise your communications, if they haven't already. Biggest of these by far are interactive television and electronic communication over the World Wide Web – the Internet.

Annual reports you can interrogate

You won't need to be told that the Internet is very, very big indeed. In fact, if you haven't already got a strategy for electronic media you're well behind.

One example illustrates the potential power of this medium. For years, Britain's Charity Commission has made available its public register of approved charities. The public can access it by post or telephone when seeking a copy of any charity's published annual report and accounts. Until a short while ago, requests for this information ran into the low hundreds each month.

The Commission placed the register on their website and now records 74,000 hits per month and rising – clear evidence that the public is increasingly expecting and using on-line information. If it leads to more people asking for and using our annual reports, this is great news for the not-for-profit communicator.

But how should you use this most intangible, highly hyped medium? Will you have to prepare an electronic version of your annual report? Will it cost more, and take much more managing?

The answer is maybe, and maybe not. It depends on how you wish to communicate. According to Jason Potts, Head of New Media at the Burnett Associates Group, the added value offered by the Internet is its interactivity. The Net enables you to offer your audiences choices in a far more flexible way than is possible with the printed page.

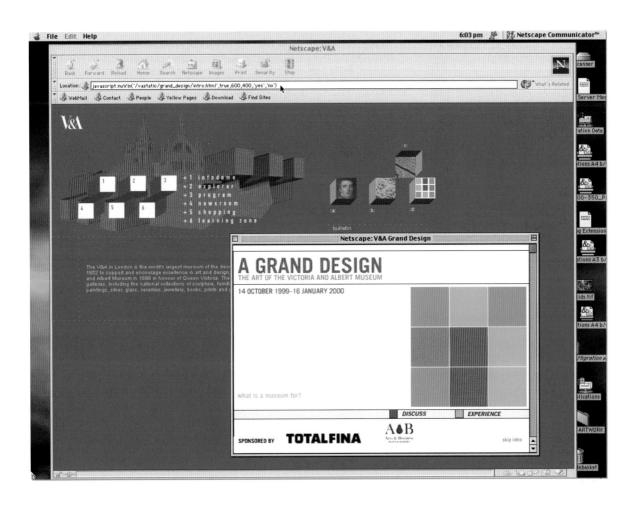

As a minimum you can post static pages from your publications on your website and offer your readers the choice of a paper or a paperless report. You can also put all the financial detail and lists of committees, too boring or long for your printed annual review on your website, so they are easily accessible for those who want them. But interactivity is the Internet's strength. The annual report that can be interrogated isn't far away.

For the first time the entire sum of human knowledge is searchable. If your annual report is in there too you can make sure that anyone looking for any subject that's a priority for you will be picked up so your information will then be available for them. The potential to interest, involve and inspire new readers is almost boundless.

Before long, so we're told, everyone's television will be interactive and on-line. The over-50s, prime among target groups for not-for-profits, are in the vanguard of this communications

▲ 3-D interactive technology and very strong graphics give the V&A an appropriate and involving site. But because a good website is dynamic, even a very good one looks dull on the printed page. www.vam.ac.uk

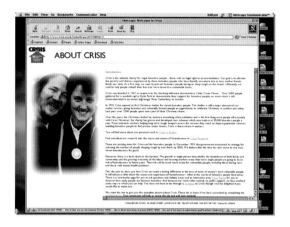

▲ Crisis' website reflects their corporate style and uses interactive key words within the copy.
www.crisis.org.uk

Other websites worth checking out:

- **www.greenpeace.org** Probably the most visited not-for-profit website, check out the ICQ button on the donation form, a neat bit of customer service.

- **www.redcross.org** Probably the most successful fundraising site around, raising in the millions of dollars.

- **www.greenpeace.org.uk** Nicely designed, plenty going on.

- **www.shelter.org.uk** Simple, clear, easy to find your way around.

revolution. So the entrepreneurial not-for-profit communicator will not be slow to understand and take advantage of it too.

The on-line video report is coming

An understanding of and a dialogue with supporters is essential. How do your existing audiences wish to receive information? What choices can you give for people to decide what information they would like and what they will pass over? How can electronic communication reinforce your publications, and vice versa?

Nothing moves people like sound and vision, so you might offer your supporters a video they can download or view on-line. Some readers might welcome e-mail updates on selected key issues from your report. Direct dialogue with supporter services could be a boon for some readers, and a fundraising and relationship building opportunity for you. On-line Q&A sessions with your legacy adviser might be widely appreciated and vastly profitable. And an on-line chat room once a month with your chief executive officer might at last add some meaning and value to the ubiquitous director's message. Then of course there are campaigning and fundraising applications such as petitions, letter-writing, on-line direct debits, Gift Aid and so on. The possibilities of electronic communication are as varied and flexible as your imagination will allow.

Remember that in this area nothing stays static for long. The percentage of regular surfers on your current database may have multiplied rapidly long before your next annual survey of supporters' reading habits.

Do it yourself?

Gifted amateurs can do a surprising amount of web production themselves. If technical help is needed there are specialist agencies who operate as capacity builders, helping not-for-profit organisations to plan and implement their strategies and develop in-house skills that will enable them to maintain and maximise their electronic communications themselves.

For most organisations, more sophisticated uses may indeed require substantial outlay and it is possible to spend large sums utilising the web. But returns from electronic communication should be easily and quickly quantifiable so you can increase or decrease your exposure as needs change and situations demand.

© Mat Wright

2 Making the most of the opportunity

You have to produce an annual report. So why not make it worth its weight in gold? Think of it as a shop window for your organisation – one that can catch the attention of your readers and make them want to come inside. Think of it as a chance to clear up any misconceptions about your organisation. Think of it as a strategic tool which can take your organisation forward in its goals. Think of it as an opportunity. ▶

Wonderful images of dogs are used in the Dogs' Home Manchester annual review 1998/99 to stop animal lovers in their tracks.

'The annual report and accounts should be more than an historical financial benchmark – they should also be seen as a public relations tool.'

Pesh Framjee, Head of the Charity Unit at Binder Hamlyn and Arthur Andersen, and a member of the SORP (Statement of Recommended Practice) Review Committee.

▲ **Your formal annual report and accounts documents don't have to be dry and boring. The NSPCC added warm pictures of children and moving case histories to its formal feedback in order to bring the need for the NSPCC's work home to readers in a very human way.**

More than just an annual report

Your annual report has to fulfil certain legal requirements. But how you present that information and what you add to it in order to make it more interesting, inviting and helpful for your readers is up to you.

Annual report or annual review? Or both?

Your statutory obligation is to produce full, audited accounts which meet SORP regulations (see page 25), together with a trustees' statement outlining the aims, progress, challenges and achievements of your organisation over the year, plus some indication of strategic direction and future plans. These must be submitted to the Charity Commission and be available, free of charge, to anyone who wants them.

Whether your target reader will be grabbed by this often rather dry document is another matter. So think carefully about the best way of telling them about what your organisation has been up to. Can you, for example, add human interest and colour to your statutory annual report document? Case histories or profiles of new projects – set apart from the required statements so that they catch the eye – can help anchor your statistics to real life and give them a more tangible meaning.

Can you add a warm and vibrant annual review that gives readers feedback on how their support has made a measurable impact on the need you serve, or may do so in the future? You can include a summary of your audited accounts, notes to explain what they mean, and a contact number for ordering the full report and accounts, or a pocket containing them at the back if they aren't too unwieldy. This statutory element can be produced very cheaply and only given to the Charity Commission and those people who ask for it, primarily companies and trusts.

It is also good practice to consider making your annual report available in other formats (eg audio cassette, computer disk) if requested. In this way, you can be sure of complying with the DDA (see panel opposite).

A shop window for your organisation

Whatever shape it takes, use your annual report or review as a shop window to set out your current work, values and products. Have this image at the front of your mind when planning what you need in order to capture the attention of your potential customers as they walk by with a hundred and one things on their minds.

How can you make your shop front look appealing? Which products should you show to pull the reader inside? How can you then offer a warm welcome, help and relevant information? What will make your customer buy something, or come back in the future? Once you get your readers into your publication, seize the opportunity!

A way of thanking your donors …

You owe it to your donors, and perhaps your volunteers, to tell them how you used their support and what difference it has made against the need.

… and soliciting further support

If your donors are in fact paying for your annual report or review, you also owe it to them to maximise the opportunity and use it to raise more support for the cause they wanted to help. So make sure you build in a message of current and future unmet need, as well as achievement. And make it crystal clear that the readers' involvement is central to your ability to help homeless youngsters, rescue stray kittens, find a treatment for a genetic condition, build a new library, put on a new production …

Answer questions before they arise

The British public has become more cynical about charities. People are constantly asking why organisations working in the same field don't merge to pool their resources and expertise, why charities have so much money in the bank, or whether they are fundraising mainly to support a huge bureaucracy.

Don't be afraid of tackling difficult issues. Use your annual report to explain your position and justify it if you believe it is right (see page 22).

Look to the future

Both your statutory report and accounts, and your 'shop window' report or review, should include some reference to the future. What challenges is your organisation facing? How will you rise to them? What new initiatives are planned? What is the role of the reader in this scenario? Look back, yes, but remember to look forward too. This is your flagship publication – make the most of it!

Purpose of a charity annual report and accounts

- The purpose of preparing a charity's annual report and accounts is to discharge the charity trustees' duty of public accountability and stewardship.

- The report and accounts should:

  (a) Provide timely and regular information on the charity and its funds.

  (b) Enable the reader to gain an understanding of the charity's activities and achievements.

  (c) Enable the reader to gain a full and proper appreciation of the charity's financial transactions during the year and of the position of its funds at the year-end.

From **Accounting by Charities: the Statement of Recommended Practice**, Charity Commission, 1995.

Disability Discrimination Act

An October 1999 update to the DDA requires all organisations to make reasonable adjustments to all goods, facilities and services so they are accessible to people with disabilites. See the DDA's Code of Practice www.disability.gov.uk or call the DDA helpline on 0345 622 633.

Answering to the people who use your services

Most annual reports are written with funders in mind. This is absolutely right. However, few also seek to communicate through their annual report with the people who **use** their services. This is almost certainly short-sighted.

John Stoker, Chief Charity Commissioner, points out the danger. 'In an age when every individual is encouraged to recognise and use their 'rights', 'beneficiaries' have developed expectations of charities which promote themselves and raise money on the platform of helping them. If a vulnerable person feels that he or she is being let down and feels strongly enough to shout about it, the damage to the charity could be devastating.'

Being accountable on all fronts will become the rule in the future. Act now and you can lead the way.

This is the information age

Thanks to the requirements of the SORP, and to the Internet, people can seek out information about charities' affairs in a way they have never been able to before.

At the time of going to press, more than 70,000 people a month are accessing the Charity Commission's register of charities. A significant number may then ask for accounts and if the figures don't add up, or look unusual – even if it's for a very good reason – you can be sure it will be spotted.

So take the initiative and explain the situation in your annual report.

Explain before you are asked: the new accountability

Many not-for-profit organisations have traditionally concentrated in their annual reports on telling the reader their good news. And there is a tremendous amount of good stuff to report back on. But they have also shied away from tackling difficult issues. Some may have relied on the goodwill of the public not to ask questions. Others – particularly small organisations – may have thought no one would notice.

But in today's Britain, this is a dangerous – if not plain daft – approach. Good intentions on the part of charities are no longer enough. If you are asking people for donations, large or small, you have to expect them to want to know exactly what their money is needed for, that you will spend it well, and that it will actually make a positive and lasting impact on that need. If you don't offer this information, the public and journalists can and will now go out and get it themselves and then interpret it in their own way. You can't blame them, can you?

As John Stoker, Chief Charity Commissioner, says, 'Trustees need to see the potential damage that can be caused if people challenge them simply because they haven't explained something properly, for example, what their reserves are for. An investment in fundraising and administration is most probably legitimate and will vary enormously between organisations, depending on what they do, but the amounts spent need to be explained not glossed over or hidden away.'

Show you have nothing to hide

Don't underestimate the new power of accountability. Voluntary organisations are increasingly expected to be open and transparent, to have clearly identified and measured the need they are addressing, and to be able to measure their progress against that need. The key question for your annual report is not so much how much money has been *spent* on your aims, but how much has been *achieved* with that money.

The organisation that takes the initiative to be accountable, therefore, rather than waiting to be coerced into disclosures, will be the one that gains an advantage over its competitors.

the standards we set ourselves

ActionAid's staff and Trustees work together to ensure that the principles of quality, impartiality and legality govern everything we do. In addition, we operate specific standards in key areas of our work.

Running projects effectively

New country programmes are subject to agreement by the independent Board of Trustees and individual projects are designed in conjunction with local people to make sure that effort is focused where it will make a real difference.

Our staff are predominantly drawn from the countries in which we work, not only ensuring understanding of local conditions but building indigenous capacity and expertise.

Being open and accountable

Supporters' funds are strictly earmarked and tied to the purpose of the donation. If conditions change and this purpose cannot be achieved, we seek supporters' permission to switch to a different project.

ActionAid publishes details of its entire salary range in its financial statements, going beyond the minimum disclosure requirements. Salaries are set at the minimum level necessary to secure the services of the best person for the job.

We monitor and disclose supporter complaint levels – for example, in 1998 we received just 673 complaints from over 124,000 UK supporters.

Looking after the money

Fundraising investment by ActionAid generated five times its volume in income for our work in 1998 (ratio of fundraising spending to incoming resources).

We operate strict 'return on investment' criteria for all fundraising activity to maximise the funds that are available for our projects.

We do not believe in building up unnecessary levels of reserves – we aim to keep them at a prudent minimum, sufficient to cover at least three months of the following year's planned spending on long-term commitments.

Looking after our supporters

ActionAid enjoys excellent supporter loyalty – on average our sponsors continue their support for eight years.

All supporters receive regular reports on how their funds are used. In addition we always aim to respond to any complaints with a specific reply within 48 hours.

We protect our sponsors from mailshots by operating a policy of refusing to sell or exchange mailing lists with their details to other organisations.

Our vision

ActionAid's vision is a world without poverty in which everyone can exercise their right to a life of dignity.

Our mission

ActionAid's mission is to work with poor and marginalised people to eradicate poverty by overcoming the injustice and inequity that cause it.

The ActionAid family

ActionAid
Hamlyn House,
Macdonald Road,
London N19 5PG, UK
Tel: 020 7561 7561
Fax: 020 7272 0899
Email: mail@actionaid.org.uk
Website: www.actionaid.org

ActionAid is a registered charity no. 274467 and a company limited by guarantee registered in England and Wales no. 1295174

ActionAid Hellas
1 Amynda Street, 11635,
Pagrati, Athens, Greece

ActionAid Ireland
Unity Buildings
16/17 Lower O'Connell Street
Dublin 1, Ireland

Aide et Action
53 Boulevard de Charonne
5545 Paris, France

Ayuda en Acción
Calle Infantas 38
28004 Madrid, Spain

Azione Aiuto
Via Paleocapa 1,
20121 Milan, Italy

Cover and feature border photos: Liba Taylor, Jenny Matthews, Steve Morgan, Nurjahan Chaklader, Augusto Ordoñez, Adrian Arbib, Dave Clark, Colin Baker, Marc Böttcher, Alan Johnson, Elaine Duigenan, Pablo Alcalde, Ana-Cecelia Gonzalez, Mike Goldwater, Andy Hall.

ACTIONAID

◀ ActionAid has taken a very positive stance on making itself accountable to the public. 'We want to encourage the public to ask questions of charities before they donate,' says Sue Davidson, Head of Communications at ActionAid. 'We've included a checklist of standards in our annual report. As far as we know, no other charity takes this approach. We want to encourage this 'charity health check' to help the public choose who to support.'

It's not enough to **say** you do good. If people are going to give you their money, you have to **prove** it.

Traidcraft's Social Accounts 1998 may not be gripping to look at, but they are packed with clear targets for bringing about change, and illustrations of how the organisation has done against those targets.

▼

Supplier Indicators

Number of products meeting fair trade criteria

Aim:
100% of Traidcraft plc's food and beverages match the company's sourcing criteria by the year 2000.

Comment:
The graph opposite shows the continued improvement made in sourcing foods and beverages which meet Traidcraft's Food Purchasing Policy. The actual number of products not meeting the strengthened fair trade criteria has declined from 44 in 1994/95 to only 5 in 1997/98.

Copies of the food purchasing policy are available on request from Traidcraft Customer Services.

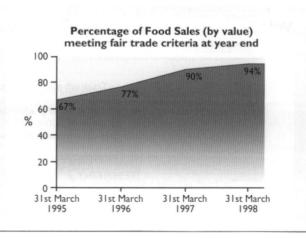

Percentage of Food Sales (by value) meeting fair trade criteria at year end

67% at 31st March 1995; 77% at 31st March 1996; 90% at 31st March 1997; 94% at 31st March 1998.

What are funders looking for today?

It's not enough just to present what's easy. Today, most funders are looking for tangible evidence of proper stewardship of funds and that funds are being used to maximum effect. That means:

- A shift **away** from measuring performance in terms of how much or how little income goes on administration and other overheads.

- A shift **towards** measuring performance in terms of what impact an organisation is making against clearly identified goals and targets.

This requires a lot of information seeking, which must be built into all your systems – not just thought about when it's annual report time!

▲
Accounts, like accountants, don't have to be boring.

A statutory report and accounts with ooMPH!

The trustees' report and audited accounts form the statutory requirement for giving your annual feedback to the world, and are governed by the Statement of Recommended Practice (SORP).

Sadly, their primary legal duty to provide a full and open account of the activities and transactions of the charity has often been used to excuse their shortcomings as an inspirational and effective means of communication.

This is sometimes because the finance director still bears responsibility for their production. The financial people can be forgiven for this, as communication and marketing are rarely their forte, but it does not stand up as an apology to the public for producing a dull and introspective report.

Involve your financial whizzes in drawing out the financial figures, messages and explanations, but give someone with communication skills the job of directing the publication. With thought, and an understanding of your target audience, even your formal trustees' statement and accounts can and should have oomph.

What should be in there?

Your statutory annual report and accounts, in addition to including basic requirements such as details of trustees, should be built around three key elements.

● **Your organisation's objectives**
What need is there for your charity, what is it seeking to achieve, and how? Explain the policies adopted by the trustees to fulfil their objectives, and clarify any changes in them.

● **A review of developments, activities and achievements**
This should enable your reader to make some judgement about the effectiveness of your organisation. Give the story behind the pounds and pence you are presenting.

Succinctly describe the progress of your organisation during the year and set it against any important events or challenges. Identify the contribution of volunteers and donations in kind if it is appropriate.

And don't forget to be forward-looking too. Discuss your organisation's aspirations and future plans. Your report has to remain relevant and current until you publish the next one.

● **A financial review**

The reader needs to gain a picture of the transactions and financial position of the charity, including any particularly important or unusual features, and be helped to interpret this picture correctly. The statutory full accounts must contain:

- a statement of financial activities
- a balance sheet
- notes explaining the accounts (if these are written by an accountant, consider rewriting them in plain English).

If you are producing summarised accounts as well, for example for a warmer annual review, don't assume that everyone is familiar with accounting jargon. Spell out what reserves are for. Bring your income to life and link it to what it has bought – if, for example, you have a gorgeous picture of a dance production made possible by a company donation, show it.

Summarised accounts must also adhere to the SORP. You must make clear:

- that this is a summary only and may not cover everything in the full accounts
- how the full accounts can be obtained
- that the full accounts have been submitted to the Charity Commission (and Companies House if relevant)
- that the summarised accounts have been approved by the trustees and ensure that:
  – they are dated, and
  – an auditors' statement signing off the summarised accounts is included nearby.

It sounds obvious – but many charities fall down here. Summarised accounts should refer to the same period, use the same figures and be prepared on the same assumptions as the full accounts.

How you can build on it

It is sadly not an exaggeration to say that many trustees' statements are dry, impenetrable tomes, with little to do with the readers' interests and needs and everything to do with internal priorities and egos. If yours is one of them, it is time for a rethink if you want to keep up with the competition.

The SORP – what it means

The Statement of Recommended Practice (SORP) applies to all charities regardless of their size, constitution or complexity, except where a more specialised SORP exists, for example for higher education institutions and registered housing associations.

It sets out recommendations on the way in which a charity should report annually on the resources entrusted to it, and the activities it undertakes. It does not say that the formal trustees' report must be long and turgid!

A charity's accounts and accounting practices must comply fully with the SORP. If for any reason they do not, this should be clearly identified in the notes to the accounts and explained fully.

To obtain a copy of the SORP, free of charge, call the Charity Commission on 0870 333 0123.

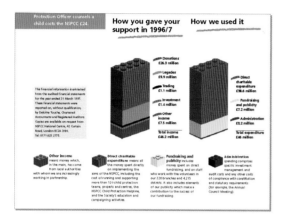

▲

The NSPCC used Lego bricks to illustrate its income and expenditure in its 1997 annual review.

AMREF's 1999 annual review used very clearly labelled, colourful pie-charts to illustrate its summary accounts, with helpful notes to explain what each category meant. ▶

Making money matters easy

There are many ways in which you can make financial information more inviting, relevant and easy to understand.

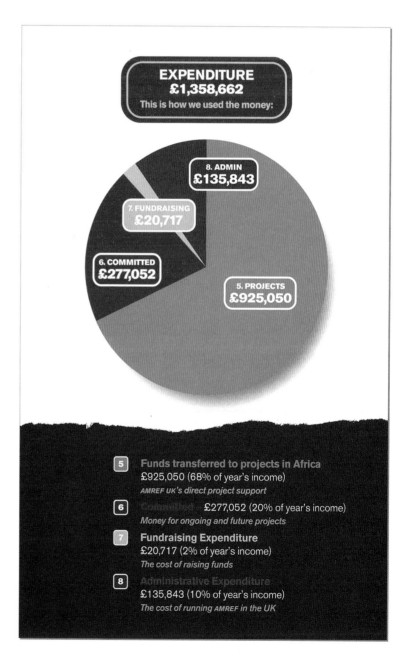

EXPENDITURE £1,358,662
This is how we used the money:

8. ADMIN £135,843

7. FUNDRAISING £20,717

6. COMMITTED £277,052

5. PROJECTS £925,050

5 Funds transferred to projects in Africa
£925,050 (68% of year's income)
AMREF UK's direct project support

6 Committed £277,052 (20% of year's income)
Money for ongoing and future projects

7 Fundraising Expenditure
£20,717 (2% of year's income)
The cost of raising funds

8 Administrative Expenditure
£135,843 (10% of year's income)
The cost of running AMREF in the UK

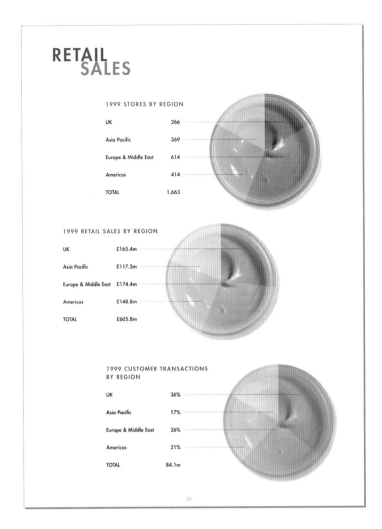

RETAIL SALES

1999 STORES BY REGION

UK	266
Asia Pacific	369
Europe & Middle East	614
Americas	414
TOTAL	1,663

1999 RETAIL SALES BY REGION

UK	£165.4m
Asia Pacific	£117.2m
Europe & Middle East	£174.4m
Americas	£148.8m
TOTAL	£605.8m

1999 CUSTOMER TRANSACTIONS BY REGION

UK	36%
Asia Pacific	17%
Europe & Middle East	26%
Americas	21%
TOTAL	84.1m

20

Financial report for 1997

Incoming resources £3,236,578

Subscriptions, donations and legacies £941,906
Homes income (fees and grants) £2,098,131
Investment income £196,541

Outgoing resources £3,304,536

Homes £2,495,090
Welfare £491,654
Fundraising and publicity £202,203
Management and administration £115,589

Net outgoing resources £67,958
Other recognised gains £436,691
Net movement in funds £368,733

▲

In 1998, TBF: the teacher support network used colourful sticks of chalk as a design feature to illuminate its financial figures.

◀

Everyone knows the Body Shop's pots of potions. Here they are used to bold visual effect in the organisation's annual report.

◀

Many people are unfamiliar with, if not plain baffled by, accounting jargon. These notes to the summary accounts in Save the Children's annual report 1998/99 help to show the reader what the organisation's reserves mean.

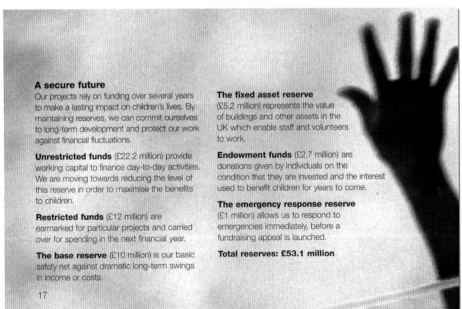

A secure future
Our projects rely on funding over several years to make a lasting impact on children's lives. By maintaining reserves, we can commit ourselves to long-term development and protect our work against financial fluctuations.

Unrestricted funds (£22.2 million) provide working capital to finance day-to-day activities. We are moving towards reducing the level of this reserve in order to maximise the benefits to children.

Restricted funds (£12 million) are earmarked for particular projects and carried over for spending in the next financial year.

The base reserve (£10 million) is our basic safety net against dramatic long-term swings in income or costs.

The fixed asset reserve
(£5.2 million) represents the value of buildings and other assets in the UK which enable staff and volunteers to work.

Endowment funds (£2.7 million) are donations given by individuals on the condition that they are invested and the interest used to benefit children for years to come.

The emergency response reserve
(£1 million) allows us to respond to emergencies immediately, before a fundraising appeal is launched.

Total reserves: £53.1 million

17

Awards: get yourself noticed

Putting together an inspirational and hard-working annual report for your various readers takes a lot of effort. But it pays. Most importantly, it can gain you new friends, new contacts, and new awareness. But it can also win you an award and get your organisation – and you! – noticed, in the sector as a whole and in the media.

You can enter your annual report and annual review for a number of awards. Perhaps the most prestigious at present are the Charity Annual Report and Accounts Awards run by the Charities Aid Foundation (CAF) in conjunction with the Institute of Chartered Accountants in England and Wales, and the Charity Forum. Prizes are awarded to charities which ... 'make a positive communication to members, donors, potential donors and shareholders, as well as fulfilling the requirements for a record of stewardship [technical accounting].' There are currently four categories of entry, depending on the level of your income, so you don't have to be big to win.

CAF produces guidelines on what the judges are looking for (all very good advice) and these are available by phoning CAF on 020 7556 1200 or from their website: www.CAFonline.org/caroa

Ruth Bender Atik, Director of The Miscarriage Association, was thrilled to win a CAF award with their 1998 report. 'We wanted it to appeal to people who knew the organisation well and to those being introduced to it for the first time (potential funders) ... We went for clear language and clean design, with real quotes from people who benefited from our support to make for an easy and inviting read – and we did it all on a very limited budget.'

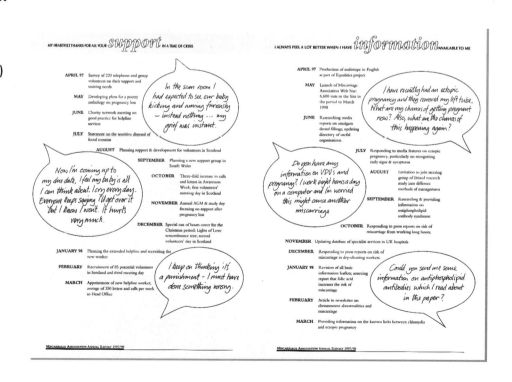

© Paul Crossman

3 Planning your publications strategy

Your annual report may be the only publication your organisation produces. Or it may be one of several. Whichever camp you belong to, this section asks you to stop focusing on your annual report for a minute, and think about the bigger picture it should fit into. This is vital to ensure that your annual report is playing a useful role, is complementing any other publications, and is worth the investment you put into producing it. ▶

The Disabilities Trust wanted to become known amongst local authority purchasers of their services for focusing on the person, not the disability. This became the theme for their annual report 1999.

Meet your reader

'We give over 1,000 grants each year, and there are only two of us to read and consider all the applications.

'We use charity annual reports to give us a flavour of the organisation and the work they do with the wider community, to get an update of what they've been achieving over the year, and what their future plans are.

'The annual reports we receive to back up an application are so varied. Whatever they're like though, they must be accompanied by their full audited accounts.

'Some are dense slabs of text which can be daunting. Some are rather scarce on hard facts. Others are fabulous and really tell a story succinctly, with the design drawing your eye on from page to page. I take those on train journeys with me – they're such a good read.'

Leris Harfield, Community Involvement, Marks & Spencer.

The importance of publications in good relations

Most publication officers know how hard it can be to secure a decent budget for publications. They are seen as a luxury in many not-for-profit organisations, because – by default rather than by design – they have traditionally not been conceived to produce a response, or to be a strategic tool.

But need a decent budget – and a decent publication – you most certainly *do*. The only alternative is to watch someone else step into the gap and steal away your hard-won supporters' attention – and quite possibly their cheque books too.

At a time when donors are being bombarded by repeated requests for money, a focused publication is an excellent way of:
- Deepening a donor's interest in the cause you serve.
- Moving on a donor to your *cause* to become a supporter of your *organisation* (don't fall into the trap of thinking they are the same thing).
- Saying thank you for past support and showing the reader how the help they gave has contributed to giving an isolated community a tapstand with clean water, an anxious family the ability to support a loved one with a drug problem, scientists the means to fill in a piece of a medical puzzle …
- Enabling people to get to grips with the complex issues you need them to understand and appreciate.
- Flagging up an unmet need which your readers can help with.

You are giving the reader something to enjoy, because they don't think you're asking for anything. Yet written in the right way, with the right stories, it is easy to make your readers read themselves into the starring role. From there it is a shorter distance to persuading them to give again, or to give more, or to pick up the phone and ask for a meeting or for more information. Publications can really help you to develop your relationships with all your customers.

What publications do you need?
You can ask a communications or fundraising professional to carry out a publications audit for you to establish how well your publications are serving your organisation's goals and your various readers' needs. Or you can do it yourself, in which case set out

your key publications on a table and write down on post-it notes:
- who each publication is aimed at
- what the key messages are
- what the purpose of the publication is.

Include your annual report or review. How is it used? Does it have its own role? What is it? If it is simply being produced 'because we have to do it', what role could it usefully fulfil? If it is duplicating another publication, could you combine them – and perhaps their budgets – in some way?

Next, involve the key people in your organisation. Ask them about the strategic plans of their departments. What is coming up in the next year or two that will need to be sold to particular audiences? Can the annual report or review help them do this?

This exercise is extremely valuable and may enable you to streamline your publications so that they – including your annual report – are more effective and cost-efficient.

Putting a strategy together

Take another look at those publications on the table. Add any mailings you have done, advertisements, order forms, letterheads, a snapshot of your website.

What impression do they give together? Do they look as if they come from the same stable, or do you see a hotchpotch of styles? When you open them up, are the key messages and values that come across consistent and obvious? Do you have a house style for the way in which text and photos are laid out, or is everything different from publication to publication? Do your publications complement each other and communicate your brand, or are they a motley crew all pulling in different directions?

As charities increasingly borrow the brand-building techniques of the commercial world, to identify themselves to donors as *the* organisation to choose when they want to support a particular cause, a cohesive identity is now becoming a must. So too, therefore, is a cohesive approach to producing communications. Your annual report or review may be the flagship, but it must fit well with your other communications too.

> Written in the right way, with the right stories, it is easy to make your readers read themselves into the starring role. From there it is a shorter distance to persuading them to give again or to give more.

Crisis uses its magazine, **Stepping Stones,** to convert people sending a donation into long-term supporters, and to show those supporters the breadth of Crisis' services and the people who use them.

> Your brand is, in effect, an essence. It has to pervade your organisation from the chair of trustees to the switchboard, from your far outposts to your very core. It has to permeate through all of your communications – verbal, printed and electronic.

The magic of brands

The big brands – such as McDonald's and Rolls-Royce – are an inescapable fact of daily life. But even the smallest of organisations can have a clear and appropriate brand. Many corner shops have brand identities and values (friendly, helpful, reliable, good conversationalists, open late) that are strong enough to persuade patrons to shop with them even when greater choice and lower prices can be found within easy reach.

Think of brand as a person. If your organisation were, say, a woman, how would she like to be known? Would the people she meets know what she stands for, what her beliefs and aspirations are? Would her individuality and distinctive qualities stand out from all the other people around her?

You may know several small organisations local to you that have distinctive brands. Voluntary organisations with reasonably strong brands that all our readers might know include Greenpeace, Great Ormond Street Hospital and the NSPCC. Everyone knows the Red Cross, perhaps the best known symbol in the world, but the British Red Cross isn't a strong brand as few people really know what they do in this country.

Your brand identity is not what *you* would like to be, or even what you think you are. It is what *other people* perceive you to be. So it's much more than a logo, corporate livery and a slick house style guide. Successful brand management is about you taking control rather than leaving it to chance.

Your brand is, in effect, an essence. It has to pervade your organisation from the chair of trustees to the switchboard, from your far outposts to your very core. It follows that it has to permeate through all of your communications – verbal, printed and electronic.

The concept of brand is exceptionally important for voluntary organisations, particularly charities, because most causes and fundraising communications are so hard to tell apart these days. This, in part at least, is a consequence of fundraisers slavishly following the formulae laid down at endless fundraising conferences.

Causes and their organisations increasingly need to stand out clearly. The new concepts therefore should be differentiation – identify and exploit what it is that sets you apart from the rest – and consistency – reinforce your brand values by consistent presentation and reiteration. It is, however, important not to become a slave to a rigid house style. Charities need flexible interpretation of their brand that allows individuality and customer interests to triumph over rules.

The most satisfactory definition of a brand for a not-for-profit organisation is shown opposite. Strong beliefs and values are what set voluntary organisations apart from commercial brands (although many companies are now looking seriously at occupying this territory, the natural but not exclusive turf of worthwhile causes). Given the strength of their belief systems, charity brands should be much more powerful than any others. Yet there are few strong charity brands, perhaps because charities have traditionally neglected to build their brand values into their communications and have instead concentrated on raising awareness of their cause.

There is no more important place than in your published communications for establishing and building your brand.

○ A definition of 'brand' is the set of ideas, images, feelings, beliefs and values that are carried around in a person's head.

▼ The Hovis logo may appear old-fashioned but it says comfort, taste, reliability and security.

▲

High quality, integrity, reliability, excellence – all these things come to mind when you see the Rolls-Royce logo.

▼ The best known international brand in the not-for-profit world isn't a charity in the UK.

▶

From Moscow to Manila, McDonald's is one of the best known brands in the world.

Meet your reader

'Some charity publications that come through the post are so boring to look at and so boring to read – they can be very inward-looking, all about the charity and its bigwigs, and full of jargon.

'And then again, some are a pleasure to look and read through. They don't make a meal of it, they talk about what they're using your money for, and they give you hard facts instead of lots of waffle.

'I won't pretend I read them from cover to cover. I just graze really, stopping on the bits which strike a chord with me or which really jump out of the page. It can be interesting to see that the charity's doing a lot more than the thing you gave them money for.

'A lot of the magazines look the same though, and read the same. When you get something different, it can help you remember the charity next time they ask for your help. Otherwise, the emergency charities and the cancer charities – they can all run into one another.'

Rita Cole, charity donor and grandmother.

Getting the right resources and sharing the costs

If you really are the proverbial one-man or one-woman band, then the only person you have to convince of the need to invest in superior communications is yourself. For the rest of us, it will be necessary to present an irresistible case. This can be really tough for small organisations, but is not impossible. It's also unlikely to be something you do just once – it is more likely to be a continuous process.

The best justification you can have to secure the necessary human and financial resources for effective publication production is to paint a picture of what might happen to your organisation *without* good communications. This should lead to a rapid change of corporate heart. 'Communicate or die' still applies and nowhere more so than in the not-for-profit sector now. In practice, few organisations challenge the need to communicate but many underestimate the resources needed to do a good rather than a mediocre job.

The simplest route to identifying the necessary budget for the job is to find individual publications from other organisations that match the quality and style to which you aspire. Then find out from the organisations concerned how they were produced and at what cost (voluntary organisations are notoriously open, so here's a chance to put this to the test). Alternatively, take your example publications to a reputable publications production company and ask them for detailed estimates.

Provided you have the expertise it may be possible to do much of the work yourself, in-house. So although it is generally tougher to make a case for employing appropriately qualified staff than paying direct production costs, you can do so if you can point to useful savings against doing the whole job out-of-house.

Take advantage of the fact that internal costs are not always considered when organisations price new developments. This may mean the best shortcut is to co-opt someone already on the payroll – providing they can devote enough time to the project. Here the difficulty may be estimating just how much of his or her time the reinvigorated communications function might take. (As a rule of thumb, calculate how much time you think it might take, then double it to take account of the indisputable fact that everything in publications production takes much longer than you think.)

Making your publication pay

There are a number of ways to help make the annual report pay for itself in terms of stronger loyalty from donors, money raised or contacts made. One or more of these will certainly apply to your organisation.

Make it a dialogue, not a monologue

Invite reader involvement on every page. Offer readers the chance to find out more about a subject, or to contact a member of staff for specialist information. Invite comments, criticisms and complaints (according to research conducted by Market and Opinion Research International, the donor who has complained and been satisfactorily responded to will be among your most loyal supporters).

Show photographs of your key contact people with phone numbers and e-mail addresses. If you can, offer a supporter 'hotline' service (see pages 49-50). The inside front or inside back pages are good places to prominently display this information, perhaps accompanied by your statement of accountability to supporters (see page 23).

Of course, initiatives such as these will use resources. So measure the benefits and be sure they exceed your costs.

Include a reply device

Many think this is a must for any annual report. A simple card (or A4/A5 sheet of paper with accompanying envelope) can be cheap to include. It might feature a range of options – everything the potential reader might do to help the cause or organisation that has just inspired them. You can include facilities for cash or credit card donations, or better still, a regular monthly gift.

It might also be worth using the reply device to *help* your readers – have you recorded their address details correctly? Are there communication choices you can offer? Mailing preference options? Any other appropriate offers? Additionally, you can use this or any other available space for *research*, asking readers for general feedback or comments on the accompanying publication.

You can even use the label carrier as your reply form, which saves costs and provides respondents with a ready-completed name and address. But unless you can turn it into a fold-up reply device, don't forget to include a reply envelope or Freepost address.

'Communicate or die' still applies, and nowhere more so than in the not-for-profit sector.

▲

The NCDL (National Canine Defence League) used a postcard reply card, attached to the back of its annual review 2000. It enables readers to easily ask for details of ways to support the organisation's work.

> Any controversy about investment in your organisation's annual report will quickly disappear if you can demonstrate convincingly that your new-look report can pay for itself.

▲

Sponsors are unlikely to give their name and financial support to a publication that isn't colourful, appealing and professionally produced.

Include a special appeal

The primary purpose of your annual report is to report back to key audiences on your recent progress and achievements. So you need to be careful not to do anything that will interfere with that *raison d'être*, just for the sake of marginal income. It could be a false economy if it puts readers off.

But an appropriate appeal that fits in with the main message of your publication and is not too strident or pleading can be effective. Given the resistance to fundraising appeals that has been bred into many supporters, the decision to carry an appeal or not is a question of how well you know your audience, and of being sensitive in equal measure to your reader's information threshold and your organisation's need for funds. Only you can decide.

You should, however, always flag up specific opportunities for the reader to help your cause in the coming year.

Find a sponsor

Although comparatively few voluntary organisations achieve it, sponsorship offers perhaps the best prospect of really making a substantial contribution to offset the production and distribution costs of your new annual report. It's an avenue that most voluntary organisations should pursue vigorously. After all, many not-for-profit organisations solicit support from industry and commerce. Sponsorship of communications material is one practical way of supporting that has attractive benefits for both sides.

- It is a tangible, clearly identifiable project that can be accurately costed in advance.
- It looks good, suggesting to supporters that resources are sensibly used.
- Sponsorship is of obvious assistance to the charity, particularly as this kind of 'general expense' project is not something that would have wide appeal to the public.
- The sponsor's contribution will be 'leverage' – a small financial contribution from the sponsor will enable the charity to increase its profile and its income considerably.
- The sponsoring organisation can gain a direct benefit through a credit. It will be associated with a dynamic, professional, worthwhile cause. The wider and more effective the distribution of your report, the more it will appeal to potential sponsors.

The concept of sponsorship will have to be professionally sold, and on the strength of the benefits to the sponsor, not to the voluntary organisation. So don't take along last year's crummy report. Present your design concepts for the new masterpiece, along with your inspirational communications strategy. A detailed contents and structure (see page 57), schedule (see page 59), print specification (see page 90) and cost estimate will complete your armoury and enable you to quickly yet comprehensively present a convincing proposal to any prospect.

Mention should also be made of the credit you propose to offer the sponsor. Don't give away too much. A discreet panel on the inside cover or outside back is sufficient. If your sponsor wishes to dominate your report, the money may not be worth having. (This probably depends on just how much it is. If they're paying many times the production costs, then, maybe …)

There's nothing wrong with multiple sponsorships. Why not try to get a group of companies to sponsor your next annual report?

Sell advertising space

This is not recommended. Any marginal income you can generate from advertising will generally be offset by readers you will lose, irritated by intrusive and irrelevant adverts. Unless you can ensure advertisements that genuinely complement your text, design and messages, their inclusion is a false economy.

However, selling advertising space may be appropriate for your regular magazine.

One of our most valuable investments.

PRUDENTIAL
Proud to support the Arts in Britain

▲ This very prominent ad on the back of the Tate's magazine helped the Tate to offset what must have been high production costs. The relevance of the ad to the publication ensures that it doesn't jar with readers.

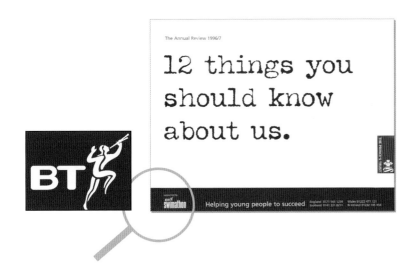

The Annual Review 1996/7

12 things you should know about us.

THE PRINCE'S TRUST

swimathon Helping young people to succeed England 0171 545 1238 Wales 01222 471 121 Scotland 0141 331 0211 N Ireland 01232 745 454

◀ BT sponsors a number of charity annual reports, including this one by The Prince's Trust. The Trust spoke very positively of their relationship with the company. 'They recognise the benefits of good corporate citizenship and of aligning themselves with young people and their aspirations. We provided a good match with those values.'

Key thinking

Here is just a selection of some of the most important things to think of when planning your annually updated communications strategy:

- **Understand your readers**
  Develop an annual plan for research and collecting feedback.

- **Be brief**
  Make your formats concise, convenient and accessible.

- **Plan for electronic media as well as printed publications**

- **Use only great stories**

- **Short copy and striking pictures are more likely to be remembered**

- **Use bullet points, lists, captions, call-outs**
  And other devices to make reading and access to information easy.

- **Signpost your publications**
  So readers can easily find their way around.

- **Don't make assumptions**
  You know what your organisation stands for, but the majority of your potential readers will not. Reiterate your brand values regularly.

- **Readers appreciate being involved and kept informed**
  Tell your donors not just what you're doing, but why. Offer chances to contribute/be listened to. Invite their opinions, particularly on important issues such as strategic direction.

- **Make financial and other factual information interesting and accessible**

- **Set up a helpline**
  Offer your supporters and potential supporters opportunities to contact you. Encourage complaints and respond to them quickly.

- **Offer your donors choices**
  If feasible, ask them how they would like to be communicated with.

- **Make special offers**
  But only if they are relevant, exclusive and give good value. Be sincere about your relationship-building objectives. Don't make offers you can't live up to.

- **Show your people**
  Publish photographs and brief biographies of those you wish readers to contact or identify with.

- **Aim for seamless communication**
  Ensure your publications function is directly linked to those who answer your phones and open and respond to mail.

- **Be proactively open and accountable**

- **Ensure your communications pay their way**
  Build in as many practical ways as you can for your communications to produce income and quantifiable value.

- **Encourage response at every opportunity**
  But don't always be asking for money. Make forms clear, readable and user-friendly.

© George Brooks

4 Getting the response you are looking for

You have to produce an annual report every year. So make the most of the effort it takes. Get it to work hard for you. Get it to score points for you. Get a response from your readers out of it.

This will not happen, however, without you making it happen. An annual report without a firmly defined direction will meander all over the place and deliver nothing.

This section helps you focus on exactly how you want the reader to respond to your publication, and on making the most of that response when you get it. ▶

Stunning images of artists supported by the Arts Council, lots of white space and very warm copy packed with direct speech made their annual review 1999 a delight to flick through.

Meet your reader

'What makes me pick up a charity annual report?

'It's important that the purpose of the organisation is immediately obvious right from the front cover, and its relevance to us as an international organisation working in different parts of the world.

'We're interested in technology and education, so if it's apparent that the charity is involved in this too, it's more likely to be picked up.

'How long do I give an annual report once it's in my hands?

'Maybe 15 seconds. No, let's say 30. If it passes the 'quick look' test I will then read the letter that comes with it. What that letter says is important, and how quickly it gets to the point. I want to know straight away why someone is writing to me and what the link is with us and our industry.'

Victor Basta, Managing Director, Broadview – technology mergers and aquisitions adviser.

Being clear about the response you want

Begin by defining the overall objective of your annual report – what mark you want it to make, what you want it to achieve. It's not enough to settle for some vague 'make people feel good about our organisation'. That is taken as read. Think about the strategic goals of your organisation over the next year, and how your report or review can be packaged to help you meet them.

Begin with your strategic goals

This will depend entirely on your organisation and cannot be pulled out of a hat at the creative briefing meeting. If you aren't clear about them, ask someone who is. Your annual report can be a helpful tool in many ways. It can:

- Create a receptive environment for a special appeal or a new development.
- Redress misconceptions, or address a particular challenge.
- Help you get closer to being put on every local authority's tender list for providing care services.
- Pave the way for a relaunch, or explain why you have repositioned yourselves.
- Introduce you to a new target audience, such as companies and trusts.

What do you want from the reader?

Once you have identified the key objective(s) of your report or review, you need to ask yourself: what is the single most important point readers should come away with when they put your publication down?

Should they feel angry, outraged, moved to pick up a phone and call their MP, or sign a petition? Should they feel empowered to make a difference and eager to send a donation? Do you want them to feel impressed and invite you in for a meeting? Do you want them to become a member or take out a season ticket? Do you want them to give their time, or skills, or influence?

To create an annual report which scores useful points for your organisation, it is absolutely critical that you answer these questions at the outset. The answers will inform everything from the writer and designer you choose, to the creative solution they come up with, the stories, design and photos you use and the key messages you communicate.

Define it for each audience

Your annual report or review is likely to be aimed at a variety of audiences with different interests and levels of knowledge of your area of work. Write down for each one the central message you want to communicate to them and what you want them to do as a result of reading your report.

Give them the means to respond

There's nothing worse than getting excited, passionate or upset about something and then not having the information you need to be able to do something about it. Or having to dig so hard to find out what to do that you run out of steam and give up.

So it is really important to not only make clear what you are hoping for from the reader, but to also give them the *means* to take the action you want them to. An integral response mechanism. A hotline phone number on every spread. An involving website. A named individual to contact. More information. A direct debit form …

 We are a charity, but we conduct the *business* of conservation as rigorously as you do your own. Working with us can help you to secure your goals. We're here to listen to your needs, and suggest ways in which we can help you to meet them. It doesn't have to be formal, it doesn't have to be a commitment – whatever is right for you.

Paula Harris,
Development Director

Strategic clarity, detailed objectives and identified key contacts enable Durrell Wildlife Conservation Trust to maximise response from their annual report 1999/2000.

JOIN WITH US TO MAKE A DIFFERENCE

DURING THE YEAR 2000 WE WILL:

● Begin restoring the central valley of the Zoo to enhance the habitat for the endangered animals who live here, and to attract native Jersey fauna and flora into the Zoo grounds. This will include an outstanding water conservation system which recycles water and uses plant vegetation to filter and cleanse the water naturally.

● Breed in captivity, for the first time anywhere in the world, the Monserrat oriole and mountain chicken, to secure their survival should their natural home be destroyed by a volcanic eruption.

● Create a new programme of workshops for Jersey schools, based on the Jersey Curriculum; and set up a Sunday morning Zoo Care programme for children aged 12-16 to help care for Zoo animals.

● Launch a Durrell Wildlife Conservation Trust website to enable us to share our scientific information with others, and raise support for our vital work.

● Begin field research on the island of Moehli in the Comores to identify the health of the tiny wild population of the huge Livingstone's fruit bat, and set up a programme to help the species recover.

● Hold the first Latin American training course (in Belize) to help conservation professionals develop leadership and negotation skills for achieving change.

● Launch an intensive research programme to determine how many black macaque monkeys remain in unprotected areas of Sulawesi and identify how to overcome threats to their survival.

WE'RE HERE FOR YOU

ANDREW FAY, Finance and Resources Director
+44 (0) 1534 860057 – For detailed financial statements and explanations of our finances.

PAULA HARRIS, Development Director
+44 (0) 1534 860065 – For gifts, grants and sponsorship opportunities.

NEIL ALLAN, Head of Development
+44 (0) 1534 860058 – For sales and marketing, travel, group and Zoo tours.

SARA CROSBY, Membership Officer
+44 (0) 1534 860012

CAROLINE SHEEHAN, Database Controller
+44 (0) 1534 860055

TRACY LE COUTEUR, Development Assistant
+44 (0) 1534 860038

JEAN ASHWORTH, Adoptions Secretary
+44 (0) 1534 860019

CHRIS SUTTON, Volunteer Coordinator
+44 (0) 1534 860052

JILL CULNANE, Press Officer
+44 (0) 1534 860026

The **wellbeing of every teacher**
is vital to us all

TBF the teacher support network   annual review 1998/99

▲ The Teachers' Benevolent Fund
relaunched in 1999 as
TBF: the teacher support network,
to reflect its new, wider focus of
supporting working teachers in their
daily lives – in addition to their
traditional work.

They wanted the photography,
copy and stories in their annual
review to communicate this change
and its relevance to a wide variety
of audiences (see opposite).

Learning from the best

The wellbeing of every teacher is vital to us all. This was the title
of the 1998/99 annual review produced by TBF: the teacher
support network. This concept came out of the well-defined
aims of the report:

● To unite a variety of readers behind the need to support
teachers in their daily lives.

● To show how TBF has evolved and repositioned itself to
meet the changing needs of working teachers, as well as
traditional beneficiaries.

Inside, every element is constructed to support these themes and
solicit an appropriate response from the different audiences:

Government
Key message: TBF is well placed to help improve the well-being
of teachers so they can be as effective, focused and inspirational
as they want to be in our schools.
Desired response: We want this audience to fund our teacher
support services, which benefit the profession as a whole.

Local Education Authorities and school governors
Key message: TBF can improve your teachers' well-being, so they
can cope with the pressures of change and derive greater job
satisfaction. This makes for an effective classroom environment.
Desired response: To work in partnership with TBF, by
commissioning employee assistance packages for their teachers.

Companies and trusts
Key message: TBF is the best way to reach teachers with positive
support. You can make teaching and learning an inspirational
experience. It's an investment in the future.
Desired response: Financial support and partnerships.

Trade unions
Key message: TBF will complement the activities of the teaching
unions and will help inform debate.
Desired response: To strengthen local and national relationships.

Teachers

Key message: TBF is all about me and my everyday needs. I don't have to be in crisis to ask for help. TBF is on my side.

Desired response: To know what help is available, how to access it and how TBF is about teachers helping teachers.

Individual supporters

Key message: TBF still provides benefits to teachers in crisis, as before, but now also provides a support service for all teachers.

Desired response: To continue supporting TBF with donations.

'To get the most out of your annual review, it's vital that you really hone your thoughts and define what the key message is that you want each reader to come away with. Then you choose the stories you use on the basis of how well they light up those messages.'

Patrick Nash, Chief Executive, TBF: the teacher support network.

Intimate photographs capture the special spark between teacher and pupil, and remind the reader of the inspirational and important job we rely on our teachers to do.

On each spread, the panel beneath the photo focuses on a different type of partnership the reader can buy into, in this instance The Wellbeing Project in Norfolk, commissioned by Norfolk Education Authority.

A call to action at the end of the review emphasises the role the different types of reader can play in supporting our teachers so that they can be the best they can be. This is followed by named contact people and numbers so all the reader needs to do is pick up the phone.

◀ The NSPCC's 1999 annual review was built around the need to thank supporters for what they had helped the NSPCC to achieve during the year, while also informing them of new child protection initiatives being developed through its recently launched FULL STOP campaign.

At the same time, by looking back on a busy year, the review made the point that FULL STOP campaign activities were in addition to the NSPCC's existing services for children.

▼ From beginning to end, the focus is on the reader and the link between what they have given or raised and the difference it is making in a vulnerable child's life. The supporter is the hero of the NSPCC's story, and is asked to continue showing compassion for children in a practical way.

The needs and views of charity fundraisers should be listened to and championed because so much depends on them: this was the key message that the Institute of Charity Fundraising Managers (ICFM) wanted to plant in the minds of the Government and the Civil Service with their 1998 annual review.

ICFM Institute of Charity Fundraising Managers

What matters to you matters to us
Annual Review 1997/8

Putting fundraisers' needs
on the national agenda

Setting the highest standards
in professional fundraising

Enabling our members
to rise to the challenge

An increasingly
central role in society

'Fundraising has become a true and honourable profession. The ICFM has been a key to its growth; its training programmes are superb, its supervision of good practice essential.'

George Smith
Honorary Fellow of ICFM

'What matters to you matters to us...'

Brian Roberts-Wray
Chairman of ICFM
Executive Committee

Putting fundraisers' needs
on the national agenda 2

Setting the highest standards
in professional fundraising 4

Enabling our members
to rise to the challenge 6

Spreading best practice
and sharing news 8

An increasingly
central role in society 10

'We're here to help you.' 12

1

'Our annual review set out to show decision-makers that professional fundraising underpins many of the essential services the public expects them to deliver. Authoritative endorsements helped present a compelling case to the reader for working with the Institute in the future.'

Stephen Lee, former director, Institute of Charity Fundraising Managers.

'The value of ICFM as an advocate for fundraisers in Westminster and Whitehall is enormous. Even large charities cannot be everywhere. Without ICFM, the implications of new legislation and policy could pass us by. The Institute alerts charities to the issues, and then gives us a channel to address them effectively.'

Ian Ventham

Putting fundraisers' needs
on the national agenda

2

3

◄ The mental health charity Richmond Fellowship chose this painting by a service-user, with a quote in his own words, for the front cover of their 1999 annual report.

They wanted to show potential statutory purchasers of their services how they tailor their community care to the individual and really nurture people's abilities.

▲ Richmond Fellowship's annual report is their main shop window for local health authorities seeking expert, value-for-money care for people with a mental health problem.

Striking conceptual photos grab the reader's attention. Frank, lively endorsements from current purchasers vouch for Richmond Fellowship as experts in care and experts in the business of care.

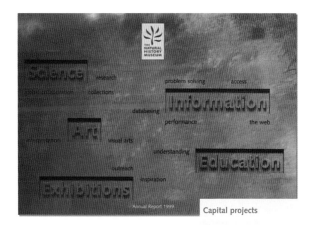

Capital projects

Caring for the collections

Performance and people

Kirsty Paterson, PR Officer, was very clear about the response The Natural History Museum needed to achieve with their annual report, as she explains: 'The objectives of our annual report were linked very closely to our corporate objectives: to raise the profile of The Natural History Museum's scientific work. We wanted to shift people's perception of what the museum is all about, to show that we are active in research around the globe.'

▲ Don't be shy to spell out what you are hoping for from your reader. But remember not to focus just on what **you** want: always try to frame it within the context of what is in it for the reader too.

Richmond Fellowship's New Business Director closes their annual report with a friendly 'let's talk', and a strong emphasis on how statutory purchasers can benefit from a partnership.

Monitoring, recording and handling response

Every response generated by your communications is an opportunity, the start of a process rather than the end. It has cost you a lot in time, effort and money to encourage this interest, so it makes sense to do all in your power to maximise its benefits for your organisation.

Meticulous records are essential. Each response – visits and phone calls as well as letters and postcards – should be recorded, evaluated, responded to appropriately and kept somewhere safe and accessible. All lessons learned from reader feedback should be stored where they can be easily retrieved prior to planning your next edition.

You can use response as part of your research programme to identify interests, issues and trends among your readers. Within the parameters of data protection legislation you should record special interests and relevant comments on your supporters' file, to build your knowledge, understanding and responsiveness to each individual reader.

Positive comments from readers can be invaluable in the ongoing task of justifying resources, so keep a 'nice things people have said' file. Display the best of these on your notice board and do whatever else you need to ensure all parts of your organisation have a chance to share your readers' enthusiasm for your communications.

Take scrupulous care over any donations or fundraising leads that your publications generate. Ensure all responses are promptly, courteously and efficiently followed up – this applies as much to complainers as it does to donors.

◄ This letter to Crisis is proof that publications **can** get a useful response.

Dear Sir,
I have just been reading for the first time your "Stepping Stones" for Summer 1999. I was so impressed that I am moved to send you a "cheque" for £50 —

Key elements of supporter service

What happens when your mum calls her favourite charity asking for information about the work they do and how her donations are used? How is she likely to be treated? Will she be impressed with efficient and friendly service? Will she be made to feel important and valued, that her small contributions are important and really count? Tests have proved again and again that not-for-profit organisations are sadly lacking when it comes to customer service. In practice your supporters are more likely to get friendly, efficient service at the hands of their local estate agent, travel company, airline or even hamburger joint than they are at the hands of their favourite charitable cause.

Here, it seems, there is an advantage in being small. Small organisations, while not quite blameless, do tend to fare better in customer service tests than larger ones. Of course the big not-for-profits can plead that it's more complex and difficult for them, but they do have bigger resources. And most failures of customer service are the result of neglect rather than lack of potential.

Rather than setting themselves up as marketing organisations whose primary interest is in separating their donors as quickly as possible from their funds, not-for-profit organisations should concentrate on being seen as the epitome of accountability and conscientious customer service. Charities particularly should be proactively accountable to all of their key constituencies and should strive to make them shareholders in the cause. Not-for-profit organisations should provide a lesson to every other business area in honesty, openness, listening to client groups and giving supporters and others what they want in the way they want it.

At a minimum, charities and similar organisations should provide a basic level of supporter service that will make all who come into contact with them feel welcome, valued and left with the impression that the organisation is efficient and polite.

The availability and promotion of publications has to be seen as a key part of supporter service. Ideally all front-line staff (ie those who have contact with the public) will be properly trained not just in general service but specifically in what publications and other communications are available, their purpose and how to answer and record specific queries. Staff who carry out customer service must believe in it, and want to do it. It will help if they can implement the ten principles of supporter service, which appear overleaf.

Meet your reader

'When you receive as much mail and reading material as I do, a lot of it inevitably has to end up in the waste bin. Richmond Fellowship's report is different. I keep it for reference. It is really strikingly presented and the information it gives is really useful too.'

Rt Hon Michael Jack MP.

Getting the response you are looking for

Ten principles of supporter service

- **Be committed**

  You have to believe in customer service. You have to want to do it. If you are not committed to giving your supporters the very best service and very best impression you possibly can, then move over and give the job to someone who is.

- **Be properly resourced**

  You can't do this on the cheap. Supporter service needs adequate staff and appropriate materials, so budget for it. If well managed, customer service will pay for itself many times over.

- **Be consistent**

  Donors and supporters should know what to expect from you, and be able to rely on it.

- **Be quick**

  Don't let your customers wait, wondering what's happening. A prompt response is a response from someone who cares. And vice versa.

- **Be appropriate**

  Tailor your response to your customer. Use the clues in each individual's correspondence to determine the right kind and level of response. Don't simply send everything you've got in the way of publications in the hope that something will hit the mark. Think first, and then only send what is absolutely appropriate.

- **Be personal**

  Use your customer service strategy to build relationships. Use your database to record personal information for future use (within the constraints of the Data Protection Act). People, universally, like to be noticed. They like to be remembered.

- **Be known**

  It pays to advertise. So put your hotline numbers and contact addresses on all your publications. And show your services people. Give them names and faces. People relate to people.

- **Be meticulous**

  Keep good records. Always do what you say you will. Show you live up to your and your organisation's ideals.

- **Be there**

  Be there when needed. The best time for supporters to contact you may be between the hours of six and nine pm. So your supporter services people can't go home then. In fact it may pay you to offer a 24-hour service.*

- **Be open and honest**

  If something has gone wrong or if you can't deliver as promised, you should admit it. Your supporters will love you for it, because you have shown you care and because you are honest and trustworthy.

* Small organisations worried at the feasibility of this advice could install a telephone answering machine. In any event, some adapting of these points will be necessary to suit your organisation. Small organisations are usually relatively competent at supporter service and can implement the above more easily than larger structures.

Adapted from *Friends for Life: Relationship Fundraising in Practice* by Ken Burnett, The White Lion Press, London 1996.

© Ian Waddell

Fifty-year-old Vacchala looks the reader in the eye in the Karuna Trust's 1999 annual report.

5 Producing an annual report that really speaks to your readers

How many dull, self-obsessed monologues have you read masquerading as an annual report? This section shows how you can produce a publication that says to your readers, 'this is about YOU and what you're looking for', and which creates an engaging dialogue that involves your reader in your story. ▶

51

5 Producing an annual report that really speaks to your readers

'When using a designer and writer to produce your annual report, it's no good expecting them just to go away and work a miracle. You have to spend a great deal of time with them, giving them a feel for the organisation, its personality, its work, its goals and challenges.

'I think it's also vital that they become personally involved in the cause. It gives them the fire, as well as the information, to put their heads together and come up with a really strong creative solution.

Philip Wilson, Director of Appeals and Marketing, Sargent Cancer Care for Children.

Choosing the right team

The right team can make a tremendous difference to the success or failure of your annual report. The wrong team, or one wrong team member, can derail it completely. As one copywriter was told by a senior member of a charity's staff, 'I'm not pandering to any pinko social workers', when she advised that some of the language he was trying to introduce into a brochure for local authority purchasers would offend many of the readers he wanted to woo, as well as the people the charity was set up to support.

What jobs need to be shared out?
Central to getting the job done, you will need to tackle:
- putting a brief together
- involving key people at the beginning and organising their approval
- pinning down the audience(s)
- identifying the key message(s)
- commissioning outside suppliers (including the printer and mailing house)
- managing the process
- researching the content
- writing the copy
- designing the report and its accompanying materials
- photography and/or illustration
- packaging and checking the financial information
- editing the copy and page proofs
- preparing the artwork for the printer
- organising the database
- supervising despatch
- monitoring response and feedback.

What qualities does your team need?
Whatever their role in producing your annual report or review, everyone with a say in it needs to have two vital qualities. The first is an ability to look beyond the internal workings, politics and personalities of your organisation, to the world outside where people are going about their busy lives and need a huge amount of persuasion to stop for a moment to let you in. The second is that everyone involved understands that if you try to say *everything* about your organisation, you risk communicating *nothing*. Less, but powerfully said, is undoubtedly more. Recruit

a team that grasps the importance of these two principles if they want to get read and you will certainly be setting off in the right direction.

Who should be in your team?

In an ideal world, your core team will include the following roles:

● **Project manager** who will be in overall charge, plan the schedule, put together the brief, commission and supervise outside suppliers, supply the writer with information and contacts, check the creative solution, copy and design against the brief, circulate copy and design for approval, deal with production issues, liaise with the printer and keep the job on budget and on schedule. He or she needs the authority (or bags of tact) to be able to be firm with senior personalities about what goes into the report and how it is said.

● **Copywriter** who will research and write with one foot in the readers' camp. This is *vital*. Your readers need an advocate to stand up for their interests and needs. The writer will work with the designer to come up with a strong creative solution, and then provide a structure for the publication, research the content, and write the copy.

● **Designer** who will work with the writer to develop a 'hook' to pull the readers in, create a design to grab their attention and serve up the information in a striking and easy-to-digest way. He or she will provide word-counts for the copywriter, lay out the copy into the design, commission photographers and illustrators if a budget is available, and prepare the artwork.

● **Editor** who will check the copy and page proofs for errors and inconsistencies. When you reach final page proofs it's strongly advisable to have a second person with an eye for detail, who has never seen the copy before, to proof-read it again.

● **Printer** who will provide estimates, source your chosen paper stock, take your final artwork and produce proofs for you to check before printing and finishing your report.

● **Mailing house** to send out the copies to your readers.

In a small organisation you may be obliged to combine all of these, perhaps with the exception of the last two.

'We're a small charity and had to produce our annual report in-house. We didn't have the design skills we needed, so we were lucky to find a designer who did the design for free. Having someone unconnected with what we do turned out to be a good idea: they could see more clearly what was important to the outside world.

'We asked for lots of organisations' annual reports to get ideas and followed the Charities Aid Foundation guidelines.

'The feedback has been great – including £2,000 from winning a Charities Aid Foundation award for best annual report.'

Farida Anderson, Director, Partners of Prisoners and Families Support Group.

Keeping your approval process tight

✓ Keep the number of people who need to approve the report as small as possible. Approval by committee will produce a dull publication which inspires no one.

✓ Make sure people approve at the right time. The earlier you involve them, the more likely they are to be happy with what you show them.

✓ Make it clear what you expect and constantly remind approvers of who the reader is, how busy the reader is, and what the organisation wants from the reader. Everyone thinks they can write and given the opportunity will pull out a red pen. Changes should **improve** the report for the reader or correct facts.

✓ Nominate one person – with an empathy for the reader – to decide which comments should be taken on board. This person's decision must be respected. Every publication needs an internal champion.

✓ You must gain the approval of people featured in case histories.

Whose approval do you need?

The approval process can be the kiss of death to any publication. Whilst it's vital to have an objective viewpoint – especially if you're doing everything yourself – it must come from someone who has an understanding of the target audience and what it is you want from those readers, not simply someone who knows your organisation inside out. Too often people judge copy as if it was written for them, with all their knowledge of the organisation's work and all their interest in its minutiae. Too often a brave and powerful concept – or even simply well-targeted, focused copy – dies the death of a thousand tweaks.

The most effective way of seeing off a derailment before it happens is to identify and involve the key approvers at the very earliest stage so that they can give their often valuable perspectives at the beginning, see the evolution of the creative solution and buy into the importance of placing the readers' needs centre-stage. For example:

● Involve them in agreeing the brief and defining key messages.
● Ask them what they would like the reader to do as a result of reading the report, and focus on what prompts and evidence the reader needs in order to do that.
● Seek their advice on which stories or projects would best illustrate the key messages and appeal to the reader.

Don't be afraid that you are wasting their time. You won't be. By putting the time in *at the beginning* you'll end up with a better annual report, which everyone owns and which is unlikely to involve lengthy and costly changes at the end of the process.

Getting outside help

Do you have all the skills you need in-house? Unlikely. Do you have the time to do it all yourself? Almost certainly not. Do you have any money for pulling in specialists with the experience you need for different parts of the process, or even for the bulk of it? Possibly.

There are many sources of outside help you can tap into, whether for producing the whole report, or just one element of it – particularly at the creative end. But be careful. Lots of people will 'do you an annual report', yet remarkably few understand donors and know how to produce an annual report that will get read and get results.

● **Freelance writers** can be a big help and because they don't know everything there is to know about your work, you can avoid the trap of trying to squeeze everything but the kitchen sink into your report and scaring the reader off. Remember though, if you want to create a publication which pushes the reader towards a desired response you will need a writer who has experience of response-oriented communication and who knows how to *involve* the reader – not just a fantastic journalist who can tell wonderful stories.

● **Freelance designers** are a good investment because, despite the advent of desktop publishing, few people have the skills to create a powerful design which really feeds the information to the reader, rather than gets in the way of it. Again, look for someone interested in getting the publication read, not just in making it look good.

Find some annual reports you like, and find out who produced them. Sometimes you'll get a freelance team of writer and designer. Agree a fee for the full job. Then – and this is crucial for the best creative solution – involve the writer and the designer *at the start*. Together. And find them good material to work with.

● **Volunteers** may have the skills you are looking for. But bear in mind that it can be difficult, when someone is doing you a huge favour, to challenge something you are not happy with.

● **Publications agencies** offer a full service from brief to delivery, or can provide the key components of the process according to your needs. Some agencies know how to use the principles of direct marketing to produce interesting publications which also involve the reader and provoke the response you're looking for. Many, though, will give you an annual report which looks good, but may not be very effective in moving your readers to action.

So how can you tell? Have a look at their work. Ask questions – who was the audience, what were they setting out to convince them of, how did they do it? Speak to their current and past clients. Using an agency won't be cheap, but if you get it right it can be well worth it. Agencies have learned from many different organisations and can pass on the best of their knowledge to you. It can also take a large part of the production process off your desk, though you will still have to work hard too.

Being a good client … (or how to get the best out of your suppliers)

✓ Give the best brief you possibly can (see page 60).

✓ Trust your team. You are employing them because you were impressed by their experience and their work. Let them give you the benefit of it.

✓ Be prepared for still having to do a lot of work yourself.

✓ Give your writer and designer your best information and stories – they can't do miracles with poor material which is irrelevant to the reader.

✓ Give clear feedback at the right stages. Explain the context of amendments and only pass on those which you are convinced are right.

✓ Good suppliers will challenge things they think will adversely affect your report – it's what you're paying for. If they've got a point, be prepared to stand up for it internally.

✓ Keep to the agreed schedule. If you don't, you may cause irreversible delays, or you may get a rushed job because your supplier is having to fit you in around something else.

What can you afford?

The available budget will obviously have an impact on what you can do, though doing your homework, being imaginative and putting the reader first can achieve miracles, even on a shoestring.

If you can show your finance people that your annual report is an important strategic tool this year, or if you can build a money-raising appeal into it in some way, you may be able to get a bigger budget (see pages 35-37).
You need to know this before you start planning what you want and who to involve.

When you've decided how best to spend your budget for maximum effect, make sure you get detailed written estimates from your suppliers. Check what they cover and what they don't.

▲ This colourful annual review from AMREF proves you don't have to spend a fortune to make an impact. Bright ideas go a long way! Photography cost £500. Design £3,000. Print £3,000. Result, 5,000 copies for £6,500 (plus a few internal costs too).

Planning the process

The task of putting together your annual report or review – or both – can seem overwhelming. It casts a huge shadow over all your other responsibilities, and it's only human to wonder where on earth – and how – to begin tackling it.

Put the process down on paper, however, with all the stages defined and you immediately have a route map with a clear destination: your delivery date. To create a timeframe or schedule, simply start with that date and work your way backwards, giving sensible timings for each stage (see page 59).

If you find you should have begun your report a month ago, you'll need to work out whether you can catch up, or whether you can simplify the publication in some way. If you've got a month in hand, don't wait. Things inevitably take longer than you expect, so make the most of the time you have. It is possible – but very stressful – to produce a well-thought-out annual report in three months, but planning should ideally begin at least five months before delivery.

When you've got your schedule worked out, check it through with the key people – including those approving the various stages – to make sure that they can meet it too.

From brief to delivery
Here are the key stages you will need to build into your schedule.

● **The briefing meeting**
Everyone who will play a key role in producing the report should come to this – well-prepared – including senior people who will need to approve the final product. If they can't come, get their views beforehand so that they can be heard by the other members of the team *at the outset*. Do as much homework as possible before the meeting on the target audience, your key messages, good stories, future plans ... The quality of this meeting will inform the quality of the creative solution you get (see page 60).

Approval of the brief
Out of the briefing meeting should come the information you need to produce a written brief (see pages 60-61), which must then be agreed by all key people. It's an invaluable exercise in really honing your thoughts and messages and getting everyone pulling in the same direction. You can't do without it.

● The creative brainstorm

If you are employing a writer and designer this is where they get together and pull rabbits out of a hat – hopefully the right rabbits if they've been given a well-thought-out brief. It's an enjoyable session and, if you are writing the report yourself, it can be a really valuable experience. Your aim is to work out, on the basis of the messages you want to impart and the response you want to get, how to hook the readers, make them turn the page and persuade them to take action at the end. Make sure someone whose opinion you trust sees your ideas before you go any further – a great idea is one that works.

● Defining the content and structure

This comes out of the creative brainstorm. The writer will prepare a written description, page by page, explaining how the report will grab the reader's attention and how your organisation's story will unfold, spread by spread, for the readers (in a way which is relevant to their level of knowledge, interests, and the time they have available). It will define how the desired response is communicated to your readers, how the content involves them, and how they can take action. It may be helpful to work up a simple flatplan of the report (see page 68).

Approval of the content and structure

Because the written description of the content and structure provides the skeleton upon which the visuals are fleshed out by the designer and the research and copy are done by the writer, it is imperative that it is agreed by the key people. *Now*. Bright ideas from the trustees about which stories should feature and which people should be interviewed are great, but if they aren't injected into the process at this stage, extra costs may well be incurred later on.

● Researching the content

This is a part of the process that people always underestimate. Yet if it is skimped on, and the content is not *relevant* to the reader, your report will simply not be read. Therefore, once the content and structure has been approved, you will need to find the best stories to illustrate your report and to set up interviews with your most interesting, passionate and eloquent people. You may also need to contact people whose endorsements you would like to include. Remember to brief your writer before he or she makes contact with the various people, so that the right questions can be prepared.

▲ **A detailed contents and structure helps everyone to see and understand what is being proposed. Only the first two typed pages are shown.**

Pitfalls to avoid

✗ Not defining a clear brief – audiences, objectives, key messages, what you want the reader to think or do, its place in your overall publications strategy ...

✗ Having a good brief but losing sight of it, or not sharing it right at the outset with key decision-makers and every team member.

✗ Not taking enough time at the planning stage.

✗ Not bringing the writer and designer together from the start.

✗ Writing copy for yourself or your boss, rather than your reader.

✗ Not allowing enough time in the schedule.

✗ Letting approval by committee weaken what could have been a cracking good read.

✗ Not championing the report internally.

✗ Not putting enough thought into getting the most relevant content for the reader. Settling for what's easily available, not what's right.

✗ Not putting enough time, energy or money into getting the visual imagery right.

It's helpful if the writer can visit a project – a few hours breathing in whatever it is you do will make for vivid copy which paints a powerful picture.

● Visuals

Visuals are produced by the designer to give you an accurate idea of what the finished pages will look like. Ask to see at least the front cover and an inside spread. Check you are happy with how the design leads the readers into the copy and enables them to find their way around it. The visuals will show the proposed style for photography or illustration, as well as the use of colour and the word count.

Approval of visuals

This is the time to get feedback on the visuals from those people who absolutely have to see them. Changes to the visual approach later on, once page proofs have been created, can be costly.

● Copy

Once the research is done, the writer produces a complete set of first draft copy (see pages 70-73) written to a word count. This needs to be circulated to all approvers, together with a note which briefly reminds each person who it has been written for, the reader's interests and needs, and what it is aiming to persuade the reader to do.

Approval of copy

The person managing the process needs to consider any amendments suggested by the approvers and decide which ones will *improve* the copy for the reader, which will help *clarify* certain points, and which will *strengthen* the uniqueness of your organisation. These amendments – and only these – should then be fed back to the writer in writing so that a second draft can be prepared. If there is an issue with tone, explain the problem to the writer and then let him or her address it. If the amendments are minor, you may wish to go straight to page proofs.

● Commissioning photography

Strong photos which make a real point can transform an annual report (see pages 80-85). If you can afford to commission photography, it can be an investment well worth making. Once you have agreed with your designer on a suitable photographer (and you have seen examples of his or her work), together you need to draw up a list of the photographs to be taken.

● **First page proofs**

The copy is flowed into the visual, now expanded to form the whole publication. Photos, if ready, are put in place. Captions are written, credits added. Your page proofs show how the real pages will look, although there will still be some tweaking to do. You will get a feel for how the different elements of copy and design hang together, and how the reader will come to the page.

Approval of first page proofs

Mark up any comments clearly for the designer and editor to act upon. Ensure your senior people see these proofs. If you leave it until later, changes can be more costly and time consuming. (See pages 88-89.)

● **Revised page proofs**

These are your final proofs, which should incorporate the comments you made on the first pages. All photos and captions should now be in place, all copy agreed and all details correct.

Approval of revised pages

Once you have signed these off – or, horror of horrors, made more amendments to them – they need to be checked by someone who has never read the report before; ideally an editor, or someone with a beady eye for mistakes. You should not need a further set of page proofs.

● **Preparation of artwork**

Your designer will prepare the artwork for your report according to the requirements of your printing house. These days artwork is normally provided on disk with a marked-up colour run-out to show the printer how your finished report should look.

● **Printer's proofs**

Your printer can provide a set of proofs, for an additional cost, to show how all the copy, images and colours will appear in the finished product (see page 91). This is your last chance to make any changes – and they will cost you at this stage – but it will prove far cheaper than having to reprint the entire report.

● **Mailing**

Few people do this in-house these days. There are companies, large and small, who can do this for you (see pages 92-93).

burnett works
inspiring communications

| RICHMOND FELLOWSHIP | ANNUAL REPORT |
| Job No P12804 Production schedule | 29 March 2000 |

	Proposed	Actual
Briefing meeting	Wed 26 April	
Creative brainstorm	Thur 27 April	
Brief and estimate to RF	Tue 2 May	
Approval of brief and estimate to BW	Thur 4 May	
Contents & structure, and visuals to RF	Fri 5 May	
Approval of contents & structure, visuals to BW	Wed 10 May	
Briefing list to RF	Fri 12 May	
Briefing materials to BW	Fri 19 May	
Research begins	Mon 22 May	
Copy begins	Fri 26 May	
Copy to editorial	Mon 5 June	
Copy and photo list to RF	Tue 6 June	
Approval of copy to BW (inc. all contributors)	Tue 13 June	
First page proofs to RF	Wed 21 June	
Approval of first page proofs to BW	Wed 28 June	
Revised page proofs to RF	Mon 3 July	
Approval of revises to BW	Wed 5 July	
Final proof read complete	Mon 10 July	
Artwork to printer	Thur 13 July	
* Machine proofs to RF	Thur 20 July	
* Approval of machine proofs to BW	Thur 20 July	
* DELIVERY	Thur 27 July	

Publications · Corporate identity · Electronic media · Direct mail · Communications reviews
White Lion Court 74 Rivington Street London EC2A 3AY UK Tel: +44 (0) 20 7415 3333 Fax: +44 (0) 20 7739 0757
www.burnett-works.com Burnett Works is a Burnett Associates Group Limited agency Registered in England No. 3892284

▲ **To produce a schedule for your annual report, begin with the date when you need it and then work backwards, leaving a sensible amount of time for each stage, and making sure that the key people will be available at those times.**

What to bring to the briefing meeting

- As much detail as possible about your target audience(s), what they think about your organisation, and what you want them to think/do.

- A clear grasp of the key messages you want to come out of your report (check with the chief executive beforehand if necessary).

- Any interesting information that will help produce a strong creative solution (eg stories, endorsements, statistics, articles, pictures).

- Written notes from your key decision-makers (eg heads of departments) with suggestions about stories from their area of work, or key messages. Ideally, however, these people should come to the briefing meeting too.

- Examples of annual reports or other publications that you like.

- Some idea of whether you want a full annual report, or a friendlier annual review with summarised accounts, or both.

- Last year's annual report to compare content and discuss feedback.

Briefing the team

This is the most important meeting you will have while producing your annual report or review. Get this right, and as long as you have the right team, you are well on the way to a gripping publication that will get read and get results.

For the whole team to get what they need out of the briefing meeting, you need to do some preparation first (see left). At the meeting itself you then need to answer the following questions.

● **Who are your readers?**
To be able to put themselves into your readers' shoes, your writer and designer need to know who those people are, what else is going on in their lives, what levels of knowledge they may have of the issues you deal with, what they are looking for and whether they are interested in your organisation, or only your cause.

● **What response are you looking for?**
Do you want supporters to feel valued? Do you want to make the public angry so they'll sign up to a campaign? Do you want to create a receptive environment for a capital appeal next year? Do you want to address a misconception? Do you want to sell your services to social services? Do you want to raise awareness of an issue? Do you want to be known and respected by Government..?

● **What information will support that response?**
It's no good saying you want readers to think or do something, and then not acting on it. Everything you say, every story you feature, must support your case. The briefing meeting is a good place to begin thinking about stories, statistics and endorsements to back up your key messages and achieve the desired response.

● **What absolutely has to be in?**
Will the chairman resign if he or she doesn't get to have a message in the report? Is there a financial idiosyncrasy which must be explained? Now's the time to bring it up.

● **What makes your organisation unique?**
It's amazing how many organisations come up with exactly the same answers! 'Quality'. 'Professional'. 'Innovative'. 'Dynamic'. Drawing out the *real* answer is the key to creating a report which is truly individual. Don't skimp on this one – it's important.

● **What are your key messages?**

Whatever your key messages are – specific or less tangible – they must be prioritised. The more single-minded your report, the stronger the message can be.

● **How will it be used?**

Will your report be used as a sales tool to health authorities? To back up applications to charitable trusts? To solicit donations from companies who want to be seen as supportive of the arts? To thank individual supporters and encourage future gifts? As part of a face-to-face presentation to Government? Work it out now as it can make all the difference to the creative solution.

● **How will it be delivered?**

How your annual report greets your readers can make a difference to how they read it and feel about it. So identifying that moment is important. Will it land on their doormat or desk? Will it be sent alone, or with a pile of stuff? Can you front it with a letter which draws attention to something of relevance to the reader?

● **Is there a house style?**

Your brand, corporate colours, your corporate identity, a way of always setting out your strapline, using large text for older people or for people with a visual impairment ... these are all things your designer will want to know now.

● **Full colour or not?**

The relative cost of full-colour printing has come down in the last decade so it's worth considering, but if you are on a very tight budget, two-colour printing can be used to great effect.

● **Are there any constraints regarding format?**

You will probably have some idea of format, even if it's only as the basis for production estimates. You'll need to talk about this, including whether you can have some form of response mechanism, or whether you need a pocket to hold more information such as your full accounts. An unusual format may also have an impact on printing and mailing costs.

The next step

There will inevitably be questions that arise from the briefing meeting which can only be answered after a bit more homework is done. Agree who will do what, and by when.

▲ **A comprehensive brief provided by Durrell Wildife Conservation Trust to their agency.**

○ When you are spending donors' money to produce an annual report, it's a crime not to make that report further your cause.

Meet your reader

'I generally read things when I've just got home from taking the children to school. I sit down, make a cup of tea and open the mail.

'It has to get me there and then if I'm to read a charity publication. If I put it on a pile, it will stay just a good intention and never get read. I'm just too busy.

'So if it wants to grab my attention, it has to be obviously relevant to me – and at this point in my life that means anything to do with children, and also breast cancer. Things that suggest there's something in it for me are the ones that work best and persuade me to give money. Greenpeace send out good information – it's active, it involves me. Tell me about organic nappies and I'm in! It's about reaching you with something that matches where you're at in your life.

'I won't open things that have tried to make me feel guilty, and I won't read things which I think will scare me – I don't want to read about cancer statistics, but about what I can do to help. In fact, it's really irritating when there's nothing telling you what you can do if you're interested. A phone number would mean you could act while it's at the front of your mind, before you have to clean the loo!'

Vicky Edwards, charity donor and mother of three.

A creative solution that hits the mark

This is the fun bit. To create a spark that makes your readers want to pick up your report and open the front cover to find out more. Then when they get inside, to make it hard for them to put it down again because it's just so ... well ... 'great' (read 'relevant').

Finding that spark takes time and imagination, and an ability to climb into the reader's shoes. Your designer and writer will approach the task from all kinds of directions.

Take a supply of paper, pens, pictures, or quotes that sum up the mood or personality of your organisation, images of your ideal reader ... anything that will inspire you. Then off you go.

● **Think about your reader's lifestage**
Your report may have several types of reader. Think about each as people with real lives, not as 'readers', and prioritise which is most important to you. Where are they at in their life (eg parenthood, paying college fees, climbing the ladder at work, retirement)? What's important to them (eg their children, health, status, career, putting something back)? What do they have to give (eg time and experience, dividends from maturing policies, influence to use on your behalf)? You'll obviously have to make generalisations, but at least they'll be real life generalisations.

● **What's their day like and where could you find a slot?**
How does their day unfold? When do they have a moment – at the breakfast table, in a traffic jam (audio cassettes can tell your story too), five minutes with a sandwich at their desk, on the train, in the bath? How can you make them see your report as something to pick up in that precious free moment?

● **What's likely to be their interest, if any, in your work?**
Do they have personal experience of your cause? Do you work in the same area as they do? Might they need you one day? Do they value your work for their children?

● **Write down key words and values for your organisation**
What images do you associate with those words?

● **Read case histories of the people you help**
Have they said something that really gets to the heart of what you do and will strike a chord with your reader directly?

● **What are you asking for and what difference will it make?**
Keep the link between the reader and the need as direct as possible. Focus on the work you do, not on your organisation. It is simply a vehicle to take the reader's support to where the need is.

● **What's in it for the reader?**
This is the most interesting one – to the reader anyway. What will he or she get out of reading your report? What benefits are there for the reader in being involved with your organisation? How can you make those benefits explicit?

Now look at what you've got. Think about what's important to your organisation and then identify how it could nestle in with what's important to the reader. Then build on it, *putting the reader's side of things first.*

Carrying the solution through

The creative solution doesn't stop at the front cover proposition and image. It must be carried through in descriptive headlines, the photographic theme, the design, the tone, approach and content of the copy, and the call to action to the reader. The fresher and more relevant the solution, the more likely it is to stand out. It must inspire people who know nothing about you, reassure people who support you, and yield up the information interested people are looking for. *Quickly.*

The following pages show some examples of annual reports, reviews and brochures which work hard to make 'their' cause come alive for their readers.

▼ The Toxoplasmosis Trust (now part of Tommy's Campaign) used their Daisy Chain campaign as the focus for their short, very digestible 1998 annual report. The daisy device leads the reader in and is then explained: the Trust's aim is that within five years every pregnant woman will know about toxoplasmosis, an infection which can seriously damage an unborn baby. Every new daisy represents one more person who has learned about toxoplasmosis.

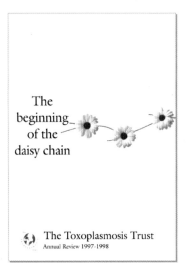

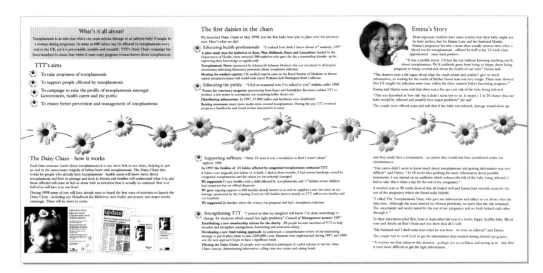

NSPCC

I'm frightened. I want my mum. He keeps asking me questions. I don't understand. I don't want to tell him rude things. Am I going to be sent to prison?

Justice
through the eyes of a child

For many children, the ordeal of giving evidence can be as traumatic as the abuse they originally experienced.

If the child becomes too distressed to tell his story, a guilty person could walk free to hurt more children.

The NSPCC *Justice for Children* Appeal needs your support to make it easier for children to tell their story without feeling frightened or intimidated.

Justice
as the NSPCC would like to see it

◀ This one isn't an annual report, but it's a great example of what a charity can achieve when it has the vision and courage to go for a strong concept.

When the NSPCC launched an appeal to the legal profession and Government to help make giving evidence in court less frightening for children who have been abused, it would have been easy to settle for **Help us change the criminal justice system for children** as the title of their appeal brochure.

But a brave NSPCC person had the courage to allow the creative team to go for something much more memorable and compelling – a frightened child's eye view from the dock. This makes you want to read on, and involves the reader – lawyers and ministers who enjoy being in a position of power – as the hero of the story.

This theme is then rolled out across each spread, convincing the readers that they do have the power and the influence to change things.

Each area of the campaign is carved up into a list of very tangible needs, which are costed out for the reader. High-profile supporters of the campaign – peers of the readers – are used to endorse the need for change in the legal system, as well as the NSPCC's ability to achieve that change in the best way for children.

This annual review-cum-Christmas card-cum-calendar from The Prince's Trust does everything an annual review should and then some more (it will be looked at every day for a year, for a start).

Instead of the expected smiling face of a young person doing her thing thanks to the Trust, they went for a typographical approach on the cover. The 12 things the reader should know about the Trust then form the headlines for each 'month' in the calendar and, with good photos, combine to communicate the Trust's achievements, values and work, and their dependence on people like the reader.

On the reverse of each page, the headline is then explained in detail in frank, friendly language (a corporate audience doesn't need pompous business jargon) peppered with hard facts and statistics to back up the Trust's message.

 BACUP (now CancerBACUP) have produced some wonderful annual reports based around very strong concepts (see page 86 for another one).

The front cover headline of their 1995-6 report tells the reader that something momentous has happened and immediately places the story that is about to unfold in real life.

Inside, a series of full-page photos continue the theme of how real life can suddenly and completely unexpectedly be interrupted by a diagnosis of cancer. When it is, BACUP is there to help you through it.

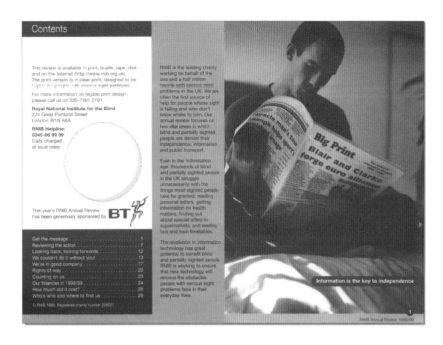

Not everything about this 1998/9 annual review from the RNIB is brilliant – it's very long and a bit tricky to find your way around. But it really tries hard to give sighted readers an insight into life with a visual impairment, and the need for the charity's campaign to ensure that visually impaired people can access public information.

The cover shows someone having to use a magnifying glass to read. A hole is cut out of the cover so that in looking through the glass the reader actually looks through into the first page where a full-page photo of a man reading is accompanied by one simple line: **Information is the key to independence**.

The next six pages then explain what this means to people with visual impairment, and what the RNIB is doing about it.

'After a recent smear test, a sealed letter a bit like a payslip arrived on my doorstep. As I didn't know what it was, I had no alternative but to take it into work and ask somebody to have a look at it. The situation was difficult for her as well as me.'

Use a flatplan to get started

Once you've identified how to make your key messages strike a chord with your reader, it's a good idea to sketch out on paper the main elements of each page or spread.

This will help you begin to see how these elements – headlines, subheads, captions, endorsing quotes, introductions, case histories, fact boxes, etc – will work together to deliver these messages to both the skim reader and the person with more time or interest.

It also tells you what information you need to come up with before you or your writer can begin the copy.

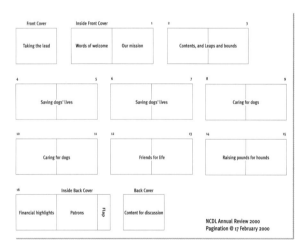

Front Cover	Inside Front Cover		1	2		3
Taking the lead	Words of welcome	Our mission		Contents, and Leaps and bounds		

4		5	6		7	8		9
Saving dogs' lives			Saving dogs' lives			Caring for dogs		

10		11	12		13	14		15
Caring for dogs			Friends for life			Raising pounds for hounds		

16	Inside Back Cover		Back Cover	
Financial highlights	Patrons	Flap	Content for discussion	

NCDL Annual Review 2000
Pagination @ 17 February 2000

▲ This flatplan for the National Canine Defence League (NCDL) annual review 2000 gives a bird's eye view of how the story will unfold for the reader. The next stage is to add in headlines and to decide on what elements need to be on each spread and what they will do.

Serving up your story in an appealing way

Research says that the average reader gives annual reports just five minutes. We think you have even less time. So you've got to work fast. Here's how you can make the most of that time.

● Make the **cover proposition/title** and all the headlines reach outwards to the reader and pull them into your story. They must say, 'Stop. Listen. This is about you too.'

● Say clearly and briefly at the start **what your organisation does**, who for, and what it needs to continue to do this. Don't lose your readers by assuming too much knowledge.

● Plan the **copy and design to work on two levels**: for the skim-reader and for the person who wants/has time for more detail.

● Give **signposts** to help the reader find their way around.

● Make sure the design helps the reader get into the copy (see pages 74-79). It should serve up **vital information in bite-size pieces** for easy digestion.

● Begin pages with an **introduction** which summarises the point of what follows, and the reader's role in it. It may well be all they read, so make it work hard.

● Use **headlines, subheads, captions** and **call-outs** from the text to help the reader dip in and out, find what they're interested in, and grasp the main points of the spread at a glance.

● Use **photographs** which tell a story, with a caption which scores an important point rather than just describes the picture.

● **Make your copy sparkle** (see pages 70-73). Keep it lively and fresh, and conversational – it helps people to get through it.

● Pull out the most gripping bits of your body text and set them as **call-outs**. If they are strong enough, they will send the reader off into the text to find out more.

● Get other people to tell your story for you. **Independent endorsements** from the reader's peer group add credibility.

● Use **bullet points** and **panels** to break up the copy – reams of unbroken text can be very off-putting.

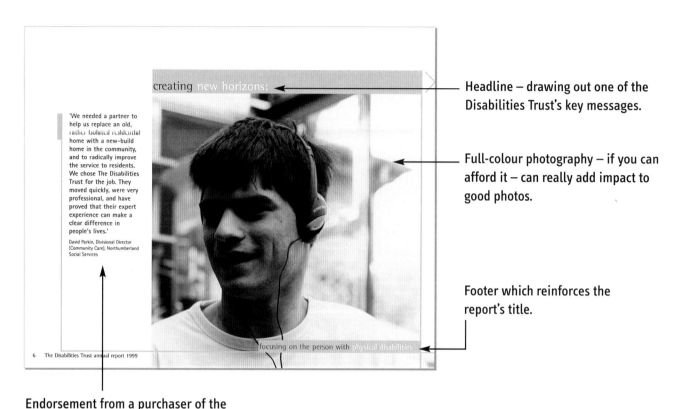

Headline – drawing out one of the Disabilities Trust's key messages.

Full-colour photography – if you can afford it – can really add impact to good photos.

Footer which reinforces the report's title.

Endorsement from a purchaser of the Disabilities Trust's care services – a peer of the potential readers – to add credibility.

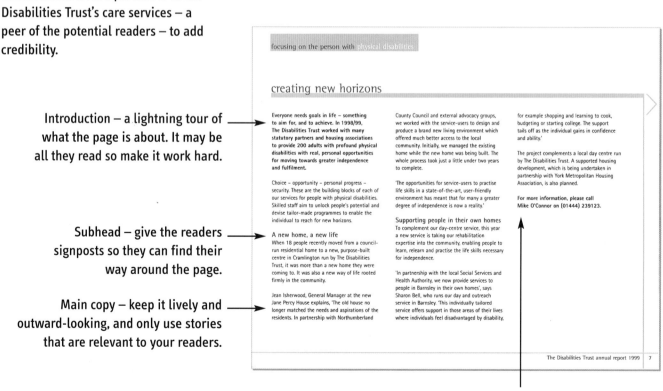

Introduction – a lightning tour of what the page is about. It may be all they read so make it work hard.

Subhead – give the readers signposts so they can find their way around the page.

Main copy – keep it lively and outward-looking, and only use stories that are relevant to your readers.

Include a 'what now' – don't leave readers dangling if they want to take action.

○ A good writer can bring your report or review alive for the reader. But they can't work miracles. They need good material to work with.

Making the copy sparkle

What makes for a great conversation, where both participants come away feeling uplifted, inspired, and all the better for the encounter? Doesn't it usually begin with a greeting, a smile, showing an interest in each other's welfare, before it evolves into sharing news, and drawing out the details each knows will interest the other? And whenever attention is focused on you, don't you feel – let's be honest – valued, appreciated and special? By the time you say goodbye you feel ready to do anything for the other person.

Great conversations, then, are involving. They also sparkle with passion and colour. To stand out from the crowd, your annual report or review can and must do this too.

Keep it conversational

So many organisations and senior people fall into the trap of believing that using the stiff, pompous language of corporate-speak will show their reader that they are a professional organisation. In fact, it will usually simply make your reader switch off. 'Officialese' is hard to read, even harder to digest, and leaves little mark on the reader's memory. Try reading a bit out loud and you'll soon see how self-important and dull it sounds.

You will make your report much more tempting and enjoyable for your reader if you speak to them as if in conversation – one human being to another – using real, vivid language to explain what you mean, rather than settling for the lazy option of desiccated, impersonal jargon which not only has no place in changing the world, but also risks shutting out many readers.

Let the passion come through

Charities deal in great causes and themes. Yet many charity chief executives' and trustees' messages would sound equally at home coming from a bank or insurance company.

Some charities have so 'professionalised' their cause that they have almost lost sight of it and the compassionate, heartfelt response it evokes in some people. If you aren't passionate about the cause you are promoting and the opportunities for moving it forward, and if that isn't allowed to shine through in your every word and every picture, how on earth can the reader be expected to get excited about your work?

Give your people a voice

The anonymous voice of the organisation can become a bit monotonous – even if the writer's good. Injecting a variety of other voices into the copy helps to change gear, keeps it lively and interesting, and lets the reader get closer to the coal face – to the scientists in the lab, the child protection worker on the sprawling council estate, the curator of a heart-stopping exhibition, the student actor enthralled by new experiences ...

But do let them speak in their own voice! There's nothing worse than sanitised, staged quotes. Keep it frank and lively when they're interviewed, and frank and lively when it goes into print.

And don't stop with your own people. Ask the people who benefit from your support what they think of your organisation. Ask your donors why they support you. Ask your fans in high places how valuable your organisation and its work are. Ask your purchasers why they think you give good value. But remember they will need to approve the story or quote that you draft.

Don't try to be clever or funny

Occasionally – very occasionally – it might work, but puns will usually backfire and make the copy sound glib or too slick. Most of the stuff you will work with is so strong it doesn't need to be sold like a fizzy drink to make it compelling.

Say far more by saying less

Many annual reports scare the reader before they've even read a word. This is often due to the sheer volume of copy facing the poor reader – a veritable cliff-face of words requiring hard hat, ropes and crampons.

To avoid the temptation to try to say everything about your organisation, write to a word count. Your designer will provide this. If there are more than 350 words to an A4 page or 500 to a spread, it is too many. And even this should be the maximum, with variation from spread to spread allowing for large photos and panels etc to break up the tome for the reader.

It's hard to write to a word count, even when you do it for a living. But get as close as you can, by making every word justify its existence, then put it away for a day. When you come back to it, prune and tighten again. If some parts of your report are being written by someone else – for example, the chief executive, or the treasurer – make sure they are given a word count *before they begin* and emphasise that if they want their fine

Keep your reader awake

- Use short, sharp sentences for emphasis and to provide some relief from the long, complicated ones.

- Ask the reader a question. What would you take if you had three minutes to leave your family home forever? How long ago is it since you heard a cricket on a summer afternoon?

- Paint an image for the readers so that they can hear the sounds in the busy family centre, feel the cold sea spray on their face, touch the smoothness of a dinosaur bone, smell the bitter stench of the dark shop doorway ... But don't be sentimental or sensationalist and keep it brief and to the point.

- Present the readers with golden nuggets of small detail which will remain in their minds long after they have put your report down. You know it has worked when the reader finds herself telling a friend or a colleague, 'I read this thing today ...'

Our mission Io support all young people with cancer and their families through high quality counselling, financial help and practical care.

Cancer strikes one person in three in the UK today, but never is a diagnosis more devastating than when that person is your child. Normal family life disintegrates as parents struggle to cope with the demands of their child's illness.

Helping to cushion the damage is the single most important goal of Sargent Cancer Care for Children. Our Sargent Care Teams – made up of specially trained Sargent care professionals and other care professionals – are at the heart of our caring work. They form part of the treatment team and give psychological and social support that can be as vital as medical treatment for children with cancer and their families.

As the only UK-wide charity offering this support, Sargent Cancer Care for Children provides a unique and invaluable service. However, there is a desperate need for us to do even more.

30 years ago seven out of ten children with cancer died within months of diagnosis. Today, thanks to radically improved treatments, seven out of ten survive. One in 1,000 adults in this country is now a survivor of childhood cancer – and this figure is likely to rise. This creates more need than ever for the care and support that Sargent alone provides. We have exciting plans to recruit more specialist care professionals and extend our services, especially to the growing number of teenagers with cancer.

The last year has been one of unprecedented growth and development for Sargent. Thanks to the efforts of our fundraisers we have succeeded in increasing our income to £5.5 million, a magnificent achievement. But to achieve our goal of helping every young person with cancer we must raise £10 million each year by 2003.

And to do that we need your help.

The following pages show the remarkable expertise and people skills our care professionals bring to their work and how they make use of all their senses to assess exactly what help to offer to each member of the family.

Diane Yeo Chief Executive

The consolidated report and accounts for 1998/9 is available as a separate document. It contains reports on the major events of the year from the Chairman of the Board of Trustees and from the Honorary Treasurer.

Tomorrow one of these children may be diagnosed with cancer.

Cancer shatters families' lives – with your help we can put them back together...

This annual review from Sargent Cancer Care for Children is a superb example of a publication that knows exactly what it has to do to get read, and what it wants from the reader. Philip Wilson, Director of Appeals and Marketing explains, 'We wanted to tell a number of audiences what we are about and what we have achieved to help children with cancer, and to involve them in helping us meet some very clear targets. When you talk about cancer, the shutters often come down, so it took a lot of skill on the part of our writer to tell the story of what happens when your child is diagnosed with cancer, while convincing the reader that by choosing Sargent to support, they can make a big impact.'

(The designer, however, could have improved readability by avoiding so much white text out of a dark background.)

"It's not just about treating the child with cancer but the whole family. So often I'm surprised to see how well a family is coping and then I discover it's because the Sargent social worker is working quietly away in the background."

Dr Erica Mackie
Paediatric Oncologist
Southampton General Hospital

In the overwhelming agony and confusion parents feel when a child is diagnosed with cancer, the needs and feelings of their other children often go unrecognised. Sargent Care Teams work closely with brothers and sisters – through one-to-one sessions and sibling groups – helping them uncover and express their emotions.

Carol-Anne was only seven when her four year old brother, Christopher, was diagnosed with leukaemia. "Mum and Dad took it in turns to stay at the hospital so I spent most of my time with Gran and Grandad. I felt angry, jealous and frightened. I didn't want to go to school. I couldn't concentrate." Carol-Anne's worst nightmare was that Christopher would die. "When I thought about that I got a tingle in my arms, my tummy went yucky and my legs would be wobbly but I didn't tell Mum and Dad because I thought they would think I was silly. I used to go to my room and kick and pinch myself," says Carol-Anne, 11.

words to be read, they'd better keep them brief and relevant to the reader. Try to keep the door open for going back if the copy they give you is too long. Offering to help cut it is a useful way of 'tightening' a meandering message without offending the boss who wrote it.

Make the connection with the reader

Shake the hands of your readers and welcome them up front. Acknowledge what they're interested in and tell them what they can get out of reading your publication. If it's appropriate, root what you're saying in reality, in the lives of your readers. If you know they have children, for example, and you're writing about parenting, make the connection. Keep coming back to your readers on every spread. And make it as easy as possible for them to give their support or get in touch.

Be careful not to frighten your readers. If they think you are going to scare them, or upset them, or make them feel guilty, the chances are they won't go beyond the front cover.

Spell out the need

Stories and statistics of achievement show how you have used supporters' money effectively. But don't forget to also spell out the outstanding need to your readers, and opportunities for achieving even more.

Finally, remember your organisation is a truck

At all times, remember that the vast majority of people are giving to, or allying themselves with your *cause*, not your organisation. People don't have sleepless nights thinking 'I must do something for the Red Cross'. They shed tears wondering how they can give that refugee mother and her child shelter from the winter on a war-torn hillside. People aren't moved by the hospice building and management strategies. They are walking that marathon to help bring people and their families the care and support they need at a difficult time.

The job of your copy is to convince the reader that you are the best, most reliable, well-driven vehicle for taking their support from A to B and distributing it as the reader intended.

Meet your reader

'I remember reading a story in an annual report about a little girl whose parents were always drunk. She tried desperately to look after her baby brothers and sisters, but it was the detail of her feeding them from a tin of cold baked beans in their dank bedroom that I couldn't shake off.

'I gave my first donation to the organisation that helped her off the back of that image.'

Emma James, donor.

Getting the covers right

- The image you use (photo, illustration or type) must be a strong one.

- A single, compelling image is better than a number of images.

- The image and words on the cover must give meaning to one another – not compete.

- No image at all is better than a poor one – use powerful words instead.

- The cover must convey the personality and uniqueness of your organisation.

- It is usual for the cover to feature your organisation's name, logo and the fact that it is an annual report or annual review.

- Your cover must speak to your reader and be impossible for the reader to ignore.

- When planning the front cover, think also of the back. Is a plain back with minimal text the best option? Could the front cover image wrap around onto the back cover?

Design to take your message to the reader

It sounds obvious, doesn't it – that the design of your review or report should make your message easy to get at? Yet a huge number of publications feature design which actually makes it difficult to read the words.

So involve the designer with the writer right at the start of the job, so that they can work out a creative solution together, where the copy and design work hand in hand to communicate your message.

Whether you are employing a freelance designer, using an agency, have an in-house designer, or are forced to do it yourself (a last resort), there are a number of design ingredients which are fundamental to ensuring that your review gets read.

The front cover is crucial

If you want to stand out from the crowd, the front cover must command attention. It may be striking, intriguing (though not cryptic), startling, dramatic, or simply gorgeous – but above all, it must strike a chord with the reader.

Once inside

Once inside, the design and copy should help the readers to find their way around, and dip in and out to obtain the most vivid and important information without having to read everything.

If every spread looks different it can make life difficult for the readers – just as they are getting orientated, the scenery shifts. So it's a good idea to keep the same layout or framework for each spread, adapting it where there is a good reason to do so.

Think about how the reader comes to the page

Most readers read from left to right, top to bottom (see page 14). They will usually read captions to photos first, then perhaps the headline, the introduction, call-outs from the text, stand-alone quotes, and case histories. Only then will most people decide whether to read the body copy at all.

Incorporating these devices into the page design can make a big difference in leading the reader around the page, and helping them to access the main points of the copy.

Choose your typeface carefully

When choosing the style and size of the typeface, think carefully about your readers and their needs.

Serif typefaces are generally easier to read in large blocks of text than sans serif typefaces, which are usually best kept for headlines and subheads. However, sans serif is usually preferred by visually impaired readers, when set large enough.

Small type sizes can be aesthetically pleasing in pure design terms, but it's best to avoid using anything smaller than 10 point. The RNIB recommend using 14 point for readers who are visually impaired. This larger point size should also be considered for an older audience. (See Essential reading on page 94.)

The leading (the space between the lines) can also make a difference to legibility. It should be neither too small nor too great. As a general rule, for smaller type the leading should be two or three points greater than the point size of the type (ie 12pt over 14pt leading, 10pt over 12pt leading).

Two more things to bear in mind when approving visuals: large blocks of text set in CAPITALS or *italics* are very hard to read, as are wide columns of text – better to go for narrower columns, as in newspapers and magazines.

A skilled designer can break these rules but there has to be a good reason.

Make all roads lead to the response

If you want a tangible response from your reader, you need to make sure that all roads lead to that hoped-for response.

If you don't give people the means to do what you are asking of them, or if they have to dig too hard to find it, their good intentions are likely to remain just that.

So use a consistent design device, such as a panel, or a caption, to reinforce what the reader can do in this particular area of work, and send them to the place in the publication where they can take action.

Include an uncluttered, focused response device, which carries through from the key message in the copy. Remember that if the response device is not attached in some way, it may fall out. And if it is integral, it needs to be easy to detach. Whatever is right for you, make sure it is user-friendly, with plenty of space to write in.

Use your type well

Look at a variety of publications and you will almost certainly find gripping bits of copy lost on busy backgrounds, or badly chosen blocks of colour. To avoid this, make sure you:

- Only reverse type out of a photograph (so that it prints in white) if the area you are setting the words on is dark and plain enough to give you a strong background.

- Increase the weight or size of the type to compensate for reduced legibility.

- For black or dark-coloured type, avoid colour backgrounds that exceed 20 per cent strength.

▲ Who would choose to read this? Designers should avoid large areas of reversed out copy, running type over illustrations or anything that makes reading difficult.

 On March 31st 1999, five HIV and AIDS organisations united under the banner of the Terrence Higgins Trust. Their annual report 1999 shows what else happened on that day and the other 364 days a year.

The unusual square, ring-bound format made out of thick paper and full of vibrant colour make this really pick-up-able.

Bold typography bangs home the stages in the 'day', helping the reader know exactly where to stop and start. A variety of wonderful images to look at, combined with short chunks of copy, make this a lively, snippety publication which doesn't take a pair of climbing boots and a crampon to get through. Lovely to look at and lovely to read.

Words of welcome

Left: NCDL President, His Grace the Duke of Wellington, with NCDL rescue dog Duchess
Top left: NCDL Chairman, Mr PJM Prain, with NCDL rescue dog Bonnie
Top right: NCDL Chief Executive, Mrs Clarissa Baldwin, with Bumble

Sharing our commitment

When you read this Review and you see the wonderful progress that the NCDL is making – saving dogs' lives, giving abandoned dogs a second chance in life, helping and educating owners and much more – I think you will be as proud of the charity as I am.

At NCDL Rehoming Centres I see our staff devoting so much love and skill to caring for dogs. It's this passionate commitment – as well as our knowledge and expertise – that will help to make the NCDL the foremost authority on dogs in this country.

Thank you for continuing to support our caring, life-saving work.

His Grace the Duke of Wellington – President, NCDL

Creating the future

One of the best moments of 1999 was the opening of NCDL Merseyside, our fifteenth Rehoming Centre – a wonderful new complex designed completely with dogs in mind. But there is much that has made the year memorable, including the news that, thanks to the kindness of the late Mrs Norah Hecksher, we received our largest ever legacy. This will enable us to improve the lives of many dogs – now, and in the future.

We can be proud that in 1999 we continued our policy of never destroying a healthy dog. I know you'll share my determination to build on our successes, so that, working together, we can make sure that every dog is a wanted dog.

PJM Prain – Chairman, NCDL

Continuing the hard work

For me, one of the joys of the past year was to see how much could be achieved, with your help. We have found warm, welcoming homes for more dogs than ever before. Our Give a Dog a Life initiative has already been successful in tackling the heartbreaking problem of unwanted dogs. And we have dealt a near-fatal blow to the evil trade of puppy farming by lobbying for new legislation on mass breeding.

Now, as you will see in this Review, it is full-speed ahead to do even more. Our aim is that every dog will have a happy life. With a lot of hard work, and your continuing support, I know it can happen.

Clarissa Baldwin – Chief Executive, NCDL

Our mission

The NCDL is working towards the day when all dogs can enjoy a happy life, free from the threat of unnecessary destruction

Leaps and bounds

There's never been a year quite like it

Contents

Highlights of the year

Thanks to your help and support, 1999 was a tremendous year for the NCDL. Our new mission statement commits us to helping all dogs to enjoy a happy life – and in 1999 we lived up to this ambitious and inspiring goal in many different ways.

With your help, we cared for more dogs than in any previous year. We found many more dogs a loving new home – and many families a wonderful new companion. We gave advice and support to more dog lovers than ever before. We educated more children, and we launched a campaign that could turn the tide on the destruction of healthy dogs. Without the hard work of our fundraisers and the kindness of people like you, we could not have raised the money needed to carry out our vital work.

We found new homes for 21% more dogs – giving thousands of four-legged friends a new life as part of a loving family.

We increased our capacity to save dogs' lives by adding two new Rehoming Centres – in Merseyside and Canterbury – to bring our nationwide network of Centres to 15.

We helped reduce the number of lost and unwanted dogs in the North East of England through our Give a Dog a Life campaign, by helping thousands of owners to have their dogs microchipped and neutered.

We helped to spread the message of responsible dog ownership to many more schoolchildren. As part of our Give a Dog a Life campaign, 45 dog wardens and environmental health officers were trained to give educational talks about dog welfare.

We helped tens of thousands of people to understand more about dogs and how to care for them, by providing advice and information.

We gave round-the-clock instant help and support through our new website, which had tens of thousands of visits in its first year.

Our total income increased by 94%, enabling us to care for more dogs and to campaign for dog welfare.

We received our biggest ever legacy, which will help to fund our activities – including improvements to our Rehoming Centres – over the next few years.

Forward thinking

Now we're determined to build on these successes – and we've got ambitious plans for the future. That includes extending our Give a Dog a Life campaign right across the country. We're already planning new initiatives to help us find homes for even more dogs. And the essential work of expanding and improving our network of Centres must continue, so that we can give the dogs who come to us a better chance to prepare for life in loving new homes.

▲ Clean, serene, but with lots of bounce, this one from the National Canine Defence League (NCDL) will bring a smile to the face of dog lovers.

Expanding their territory to appeal to the younger end of the animal lover market, NCDL went for a very contemporary, clean feel, with lots of striking cut-outs of dogs leaping and bounding their way through the pages, pulling the reader along with them.

RefAid is a UK charity set up by UNHCR to help support its work with refugees around the world.

Their 1997/98 annual review was designed like a map to reflect the theme, **Mapping the progress**. As the reader unfolds the map, the story unfolds for them until they have a full-scale world map in front of them next to a stapled-in booklet focusing on the progress RefAid has been making around that world.

In just two colours, used to great effect, it is laid out clearly with lots of space around easy-to-read text set out on a plain background. Unusual, and absolutely relevant to the subject matter. (It also folds up much more easily than a map!)

Fabulous, humourous photographs of ▶
dogs with pots of personality combine
with simple copy lines to create a
memorable annual review 1997/98 for
the Dogs' Home Manchester. You can't
help but turn the pages and smile.
▼

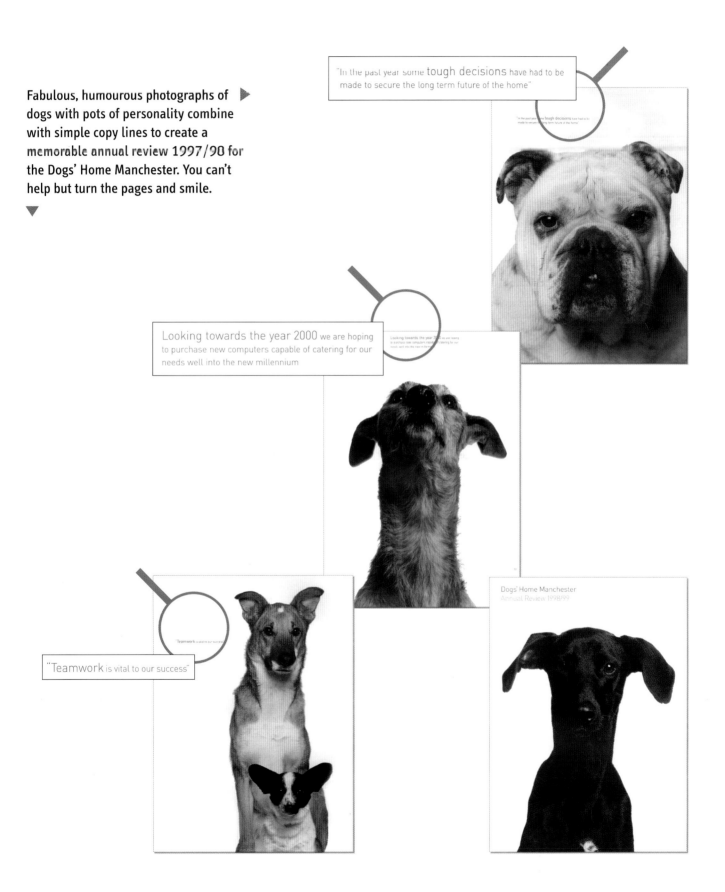

"In the past year some tough decisions have had to be made to secure the long term future of the home"

Looking towards the year 2000 we are hoping to purchase new computers capable of catering for our needs well into the new millennium

"Teamwork is vital to our success"

Dogs' Home Manchester
Annual Review 1998/99

Annual Report 1998/9

professional

enabling

caring

Norwood
Ravenswood
Giving People a Chance in Life

▲ **A warm, engaging photograph can communicate the ethos of your organisation in a second. The front cover of Norwood Ravenswood's annual report says a whole lot about how the organisation works and the difference it makes in people's lives.**

Photography can bring your report to life

Photography can make the difference between your report or review being picked up and thumbed through, or chucked straight in the bin. For not-for-profit organisations, photography offers the chance to bring important themes to life – protecting the landscape, widening the horizons of disadvantaged teenagers, taking theatre to isolated communities, upholding human rights …

Used properly, it can enable you to deliver your messages in a visual way, give a face to your organisation's work and communicate the need you are seeking to address. Photographs should never be used just to fill a space.

Investing in photography

Although commissioning photography can use a large chunk of your budget, it will be a worthwhile investment if you choose the right photographer, brief him or her well, and research the best opportunities for the photographs that you need. Even just a few commissioned photographs, used prominently, will make a big impact on the appeal of your publication and help to set the style and feel.

● **Finding the right photographer**

You can start by looking for photographic styles you think are appropriate, finding out who the photographer is and asking him or her to come in and show you their portfolio.

Photographers' fees vary, but you may be able to negotiate a special rate. Many are keen to add some work for not-for-profit organisations to their portfolios if they feel the job will be a creative challenge, or want to help a cause they believe in. Look for enthusiasm and interest in your work. Remember, however, that photographers pay their mortgages with their fees and will usually expect – and deserve – reasonable pay. You will also need to pay for travel, film, processing, making prints, and possibly repeat usage of the photos taken.

● **Giving a good brief**

To ensure you get the photographs you need, it is vital that you give the photographer helpful background information – about the work of your organisation, your values, the audience and

These dramatic photos, full of life and personality, from the Arts Council's annual review 1999 work with strong headlines to drive home the key themes of the year.
Each is accompanied by a short piece of copy pulling out a particular Arts Council grant.

Copyright on photos

This is an issue you must discuss with your photographer.

- Usually the commissioner is paying to use the photo(s) once, in an agreed publication or poster. The photographer holds the copyright and you may need to pay to use the photos for subsequent jobs.

However:

- It is often possible to negotiate an arrangement whereby your organisation has access to the images for future use, as long as the photographer is always credited.

- Sometimes photographers will give you the images, if you are very lucky, but you absolutely must remember to credit them each time one is used – this is how photographers get work.

the key messages and tone that the photos should communicate.

Do you need to portray a range of ages, or a particular gender or racial mix? What format are you looking for – landscape or portrait? What size of image do you need? Do you want colour, black and white, or both? Are there photos you want to show the photographer as an example of what you have in mind? Can you provide a copy of the visuals to show how the photographs will be used? These are all details that will help the photographer to deliver what you want.

● **Getting the most out of the session**

Depending on the type of shot you want, the shoot will take place in a studio or on location. The more trouble-free and well organised the session, the more the photographer will get done and the more on target your photographs are likely to be. If you are sending the photographer on location, go with her, or make sure someone at the other end is briefed to help her. Everyone who is to be photographed should have been warned, and be ready. If you waste half a day chasing people to have their picture taken, that's half a day's fee down the drain. Remember to get the details of who is in the picture and what they are doing. You will need to ask everyone photographed to sign a release form saying that they understand how the photo is to be used. Be sure to stick to this agreement yourself.

● **Striking the balance between need and achievement**

Many voluntary organisations deal in areas of desperate need and work with people who are vulnerable. It is this need and these people that your readers will be moved by. Your publication must, therefore, express the need powerfully and vividly. However, readers find distressing images difficult to look at and will often turn off if faced with them. You will need to think carefully with the photographer and designer about how to show need and vulnerability visually, as well as how your organisation is making a positive, tangible difference.

● **Using your photos well**

Once you've invested in your key images, use them to their best advantage. More than any other element of your report or review, they will be the hook by which you catch your readers and pull them in.

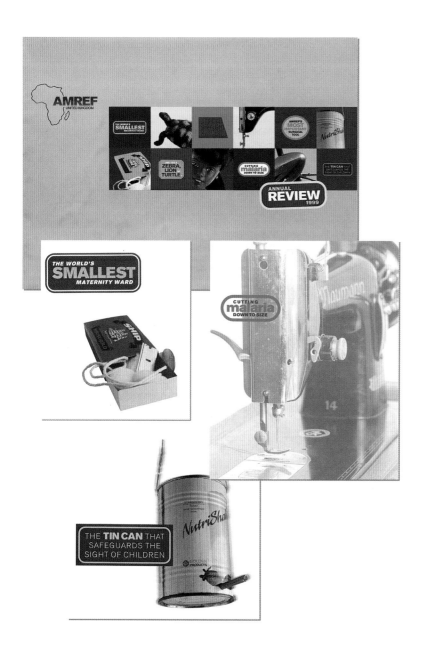

▲ It can be hard to obtain strong photos to illustrate overseas work if you don't have much money. But AMREF didn't let that stand in the way of producing an annual review that really jumps out of its envelope. Simple pictures, shot in a studio, illustrate golden nuggets of AMREF's work, like the maternity kit in a matchbox, above.

Dos and don'ts

Using existing photos:

✓ Use only the best. Ask yourself, 'Does it add something to the publication?'

✗ Don't mix up lots of different styles and looks.

✓ Ask about processes which can help give your hotchpotch some visual consistency, such as producing all black and white and colour photos as duotones.

✓ Remember that you don't have to show the whole photo. Crop it to focus in on the important bit.

If you absolutely have to take photos yourself:

✗ Avoid people standing in a line. Get them to do something!

✓ Think about what is in the background. You don't want that dustbin in shot, or that exit sign sticking out of a social worker's head.

✓ Take your subject outside, turn off your flash and use natural light rather than photographing her or him sitting at a desk in an office.

✓ Keep your subject up close.

✗ Avoid pictures of buildings (very dull), unless something interesting is happening.

✓ Try to give some kind of context to the picture. What point must it make?

✓ Use transparency film if possible – it makes for better quality photos.

✓ Ask yourself, 'Why would anybody want to look at this picture?'

◀ The washing line doesn't really add a lot, does it? Yet charity annual reports are full of people standing next to fire extinguishers, filing cabinets ... See if you can crop a bad photo to make it better.

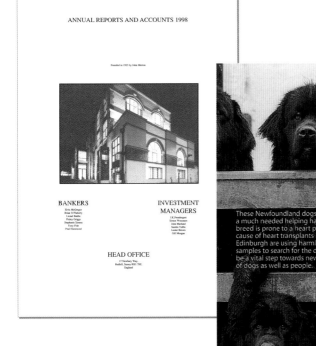

◀ Compare the opening pages of two very different annual reports. Which would you read?

The one with a list of names and a black and white picture of a building is based on the opening page of last year's report from a major animal charity. The one with a colour photo of big shaggy dogs staring straight out at you is from a health charity.

Do you really need a picture like ▶ this? Or yet another picture of a cheque presentation?

If **you** wouldn't stop and look at it, don't put it in. Conversely, if you have one or two really strong photos, blow them up big and bold.

◀ A good picture will make the reader stop for a second. Make that second count by adding a caption which does more than describe the picture.

Use it to give the reader some important information. For example, make one photo on each page about an achievement, or an outstanding need the reader can help with.

Above: Dr Ian Tomlinson's research at Imperial Cancer Research Fund aims to identify genes which are important in the development of tumours of the bowel and other sites.

▲ This annual report from CancerBACUP
uses simple, but dramatic paintmarks
to illustrate the strong emotions
associated with being diagnosed with
cancer, and how these can be calmed
by the right sort of support, information
and understanding.

Using illustration

Illustration, like photography, can really lift your annual report
or review and make it truly distinctive. But it too comes with
a price tag, especially if you go through an agent.

All the suggestions for negotiating a reduced fee for
photography (see preceding pages) also apply to illustration,
however, so it is an option worth exploring.

What can illustration do for you?

There are many ways in which illustration can enhance your
publication. It can:

- Make your report look unique and different from the rest.
- Help to visualise and communicate subjects which it would
  be impossible or inappropriate to photograph – pain, grief,
  intimate physical problems, sexuality, violence, anger …
- Infuse your report with a certain style or tone.
- Add design impact and pick-up-ability.
- Help to roll out a concept through the report (see
  CancerBACUP's annual report, left).
- Add humour, if appropriate.
- Highlight specific types of information, for example, facts,
  specific areas of need and opportunities for the reader to
  become involved.

Finding the illustrator for you

Look through lots of publications and find something you like.
Ask the publisher who the illustrator was and contact them direct
if possible, tell them about your job and find out if they would
be interested. Most will be delighted to come and show you their
work and talk about your needs. If they aren't, they're probably
not the right illustrator for you.

Beautiful illustrations are used in The Refugee Council's 1999 annual report to focus the reader's mind on the contribution refugees have made to British life over the years.

The MS Society uses illustration to ▶ pull the reader into subjects which are hard to capture with a photo, or which might be distressing to look at, in this instance (clockwise from right) fighting fatigue, how it feels physically to have MS and women's health.

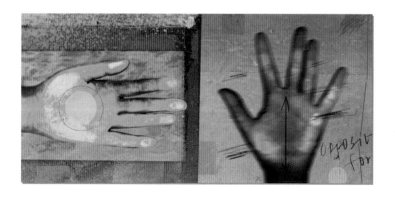

Look through your reader's eyes

When approving page proofs, you need to come at the spread first as your reader would. Ask yourself:

- Where does your eye first land? Is that the right place?

- Where does the design lead you? Is it clear? Is it right?

- If you skim-read the heading, subheads, introduction, call-outs, stand-alones, fact boxes, and captions, do you get the key points of the spread?

- Is the response you want absolutely clear?

- Are the words legible? Are there too many to get through?

- Do the photos add to the words? Are they pulling in the same direction? Captions should say something really important, not just describe the picture.

Of course, all of this should have been decided at visual stage but just in case, page proofs and revises give you a final chance to make changes (major ones might prove pricey).

Checking your page proofs

Once the copy is written and approved and the photos and/or illustrations are ready, the designer pours the words and images into the approved design format to produce real pages and spreads. These are called first page proofs and should give you a real sense of all your hard work coming together.

They provide a chance to see how the design you approved some weeks ago has ensured that copy and photos work together to deliver your key messages and story to the reader.

Put on your editor's hat …

As well as looking at each page as the reader would, you need to go through every element with a fine tooth comb to check for consistency, grammar, spelling, punctuation, odd line breaks, spacing, missing facts, etc (see *Proof-reading by numbers* opposite). Get someone else to read the pages too, as you will probably be too close to the job to spot everything. However, it is important that this person checks any changes with you.

You will need to see your page proofs in colour so that, for example, you can gauge whether words set over colour will be legible. Remember, however, that the colour will have come from a laser printer and may not be a true representation of the colour you have chosen. Ask to see a Pantone colour swatch if you haven't seen one yet.

… and pull out your diplomacy skills

By the time you get to this stage, the copy should have been approved. However, you may find that in some places it is too long. Now is the time to cut it and to agree the cuts with the writer and perhaps the relevant head of department. This can be an effective way of demonstrating to the chief executive or chairman just why you were asking them to write to a word count, even if they ignored it, and gives you a reason for going back to them again to suggest or request cuts.

Don't go through umpteen page proofs

Keep the number of people approving page proofs as small as possible and get them all to do it now. Further amendments at revised page proofs (which incorporate your changes to the first page proofs) will demoralise the production team, cost you money and eat into your schedule. So they should be avoided if at all possible.

The diagram shows page proofs with numbered arrows pointing to various elements:

3 → **Espoir**

12 → Notre action pour aider les enfants à survivre à la guerre et aux catastrophes

10 →

9 →

1,2 → 6 UNICEF

11 · 4 · 12 · 6 · 11

Proof-reading by numbers

1. Check page numbers are correct.

2. Check page numbers against the contents list.

3. Check headings against the contents list.

4. Check all running heads/footers.

5. Check all call-outs.

6. Check all subheads.

7. Check all captions.

8. Check all addresses, phone numbers, registered charity number, etc.

9. Check credits.

10. Check illustrations and photographs: are they the right ones, in the right place, and reproduced to a good enough quality?

11. Read box stories, panels, tables, charts, etc.

12. Read the introduction and the main text.

13. Transfer any comments or corrections to a master set of proofs (and query any debatable areas with copywriter/designer).

14. Once the proofs are read and all comments collated, check to make sure that they are clear and easy to understand.

15. Read proofs again if there is time.

Never presume anything. How do you know that's the correct telephone number? What did you check it against? What does that asterisk refer to? Follow these steps to iron out any creases and if in doubt, check it out.

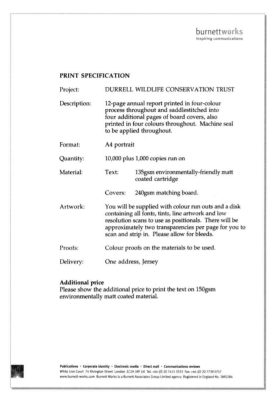

Work with your designer to produce a detailed print specification which you can then use to obtain accurate estimates from at least three to six printers.

Dealing with the printer

New technology has revolutionised the printing process in recent years and will no doubt continue to evolve apace. Just as you get to grips with one process it is superseded by another. But new developments bring many new benefits. Involve the printer at an early stage and they will be able to advise you on what's possible, and how to make the most of your printing budget.

Write your print specification

In order to be able to ask a printer for an estimate, you will need to produce a print specification. Your designer, once the format has been decided, should be able to provide any details you don't know. It should say:

- What the project is (eg annual report).
- A description (number of pages, type of cover, colour process to be used, whether you want a sealer over the colour to protect it, any lamination or spot varnish, how the pages will be stitched or bound together, any perforations, flaps, pockets, etc).
- The format (eg A4, portrait or landscape). Send a diagram if it would be helpful.
- Quantity you want printed.
- The paper/board you want it printed on.
- How the artwork will be supplied, the number of transparencies or prints to be scanned, and whether to allow for bleeds (where the print goes right to the edge of the page).
- What type of proofs you want.
- Delivery address and date.

It is definitely worth sending your print spec to a few printers, even if you have a favourite. Check every estimate to make sure the printer has understood your specification.

Preparing artwork for your printer

The days when artwork was sent to the printer as spreads mounted up on board are long gone. Today, it is often supplied digitally – the designer saves the finished spreads and covers from his or her computer onto a disk. The printer then prints out your artwork from your disk directly onto film.

To make sure everything is absolutely correct on the disk, ask the designer for a colour laser copy of the artwork first, which you can check and mark up for the printer to follow.

Never assume anything – spell everything out. You need to check:
- Page dimensions and alignment of all the elements – are they the same from spread to spread?
- Trim marks (where the printer's guillotine will chop the page) – are they correct, and have you allowed for pictures or colour panels to bleed off the page beyond the trim mark?
- Dimensions of any pockets or flaps – have you allowed for a gutter? Will any inserts fit comfortably?
- Photographs and logos – which do you need the printer to scan for you? Are special treatments (eg duotones) clear?

If the report uses just two colours, the designer should also provide 'colour separations' – a print-out of everything that will be in the first colour and another of everything in the second colour. You can then check, for example, that all the body text is in black and the headlines are in green.

The run-out of the artwork for the printer should also indicate where there is to be a special treatment (eg a spot varnish) and which colour process is to be used. You should send a list of the fonts and references for any special Pantone colours you have used.

If there are any pockets or tricksy elements to the format, send a plain paper dummy too. Keep a copy for yourself, so that you can refer to it if there are any queries.

Receiving your printer's proofs

There are various kinds of proof you can ask for. Bromides are useful for simple text documents, cromalin proofs for four-colour work. Machine proofs, or 'wet' proofs, produced once the film and plates have been made, are as close as you'll get to the real thing. Made using the actual inks and paper you have specified, they are more expensive but definitely worth seeing.

Ask your printer to dummy up your proofs into a publication you can flick through, so you can check how it unfolds and that any flaps and pockets work as you wanted them to. Most printers will provide you with an approval slip to tick off and sign. This is not the time to start adding extra commas – they will cost you.

Finally, if you are unclear about anything, ask.

And you're off...

Once you have signed off the proofs, the printer will begin printing your annual report. Ask to see a sample copy before the bulk is delivered to you or your mailing house.

▲

This is where you need someone with an eye for detail! If mistakes in the artwork are not spotted until the printer's proofs arrive on your desk, you'll find yourself with a bill for plate changes. If mistakes in the printer's proofs aren't picked up until you have a printed sample in your hand, you could find yourself stung for the costs of reprinting thousands of reports!

○ It's a good idea to give the laser bureau some 'seed names' – the names and home addresses of some of your staff or friends – so that you have a test of when and how your publication is delivered.

▲

A brief letter can draw the readers' attention to specific areas of interest, and makes the whole package more interesting and personal.

Dealing with the mailing house

You're almost there! By the time you get to mail-out time, you will of course have already thought carefully about how this is to happen. In fact, you will have done this right at the beginning, at the briefing meeting (see page 60). Won't you?

The decisions you made way back then will inform what you need to do in order to be ready for mailing out your annual report or review to your readers.

The laser bureau

If you have decided to front your report with a brief, personalised letter, drawing your readers' attention to something inside which will be of particular interest to them, you will have by now produced that letter, and any number of variations on it depending on your different readers' interests.

Most mailing houses now have a laser bureau which can do the personalised printing of these letters for you. You will need to give them (on tape or disk) your mailing names and addresses, the salutation you want used, and the groups, or 'segments' you want to break those names into (depending on which letter they are to receive and what you are going to ask of them).

You will need to give the laser bureau the text of the letter versions. If only part of the letter (eg the front) is being laser-personalised, you may want your printing house to pre-print other parts (eg the back, or a reply form) on your stationery in advance. Alternatively, the laser bureau can laser everything on to letterheads supplied by you.

Ask to see a 'live' laser proof of each letter version to make sure each segment is working as it should, that the salutation and date are correct, and that the supporter number or code is there if you want it to be.

Once you've approved the proof and the letters are laser-printed, they will be handed over to the mailing house.

The mailing house

It is the job of the mailing house to put all the items to be mailed into whatever wrapper you have decided on and get it in the post.

The stuffing into envelope, polywrap or polybag of your annual report and any enclosures can be done by machine – which keeps costs down – or by hand – which is more expensive.

The more elements to be collated – for example a personalised letter, a separate personalised reply form, an insert, plus the annual report – the more costly it will be, though this should be balanced (if possible) against how much more appealing and relevant a package it could make for the reader and how much extra response each additional enclosure could bring in.

Make sure you give the mailing house a list of which enclosures should go with which names and addresses. Ask to see a 'sign-off pack' for each segment before anything is actually sent out, so that you can make sure that the right enclosures have been put with each pack, and all the elements have been enclosed in the right order and are all facing the right way.

Then it's in the post, and through your readers' letterboxes! But that's far from the end of the story. In fact, it's just the beginning …

The never-ending story

Rather like painting the Forth Bridge, by the time you've safely seen this year's annual report off to the mailing house you will probably already be starting to prepare the next. Research among readers of your last report will undoubtedly inform your planning process, as will direct feedback from readers and any lessons learned from last year's mistakes and suggested improvements from both internal and external reactions to your finished product.

That's one of the best things about producing annual reports. It's very hard to be perfect, so your next effort will always be an improvement.

Keep your postage costs down

If you are mailing to more than 4,000 names (at the time of going to print), and your package weighs no more than 2kg, you can ask the laser bureau to Mailsort your packages so that you receive a discount from the Royal Mail on your postage bill.

You will need to have the full postcodes of all your names, so that the mailing house can bag up your packages into postcodes and save the Post Office some work. Your mailing house will be able to tell you more, or call the Royal Mail for information.

Acknowledgements, useful contacts and essential reading

Useful contacts

Book Publishing Books (BPB)
45 East Hill, London SW18 2QZ
tel: 020 8874 2718
fax: 020 8874 2718
e-mail: bpb@bookhouse.co.uk
Mail order catalogue of books relevant to
publishers, including many listed below.

Charities Aid Foundation
114-118 Southampton Row,
London WC1B 5AA
tel: 020 7400 2300
fax: 020 7831 0134
e-mail: enquiries@caf.charitynet.org
Charitable and financial services to help donors
make the most of their giving and charities make
the most of their resources in the UK and overseas.

The Charity Commission (London office)
Harmsworth House, 13-15 Bouverie Street,
London EC4Y 8DP
tel: 0870 333 0123
fax: 020 7674 2300
www.charity-commission.gov.uk
UK Government Department that oversees
charities in England and Wales.

Directory of Social Change
24 Stephenson Way, London NW1 2DP
Books tel: 020 7209 5151
Courses & Conferences tel: 020 7209 4949
fax: 020 7209 5049
e-mail: info@dsc.org.uk
Publishes books and runs courses on copy-writing,
communication skills, customer care, etc.

**Institute of Charity Fundraising
Managers (ICFM)**
Market Towers, 1 Nine Elms Lane, London
SW8 5NQ
tel: 020 7627 3436
fax: 020 7627 3508
e-mail: enquiries@icfm.co.uk
Promotes fundraising best practice and champions
the needs of fundraisers.

**National Council for Voluntary
Organisations (NCVO)**
8 All Saints Street, London N1 9RL
tel: 020 7713 6161
fax: 020 7713 6300
e-mail: ncvo@ncvo-vol.org.uk
Coordinates the Voluntary Sector Publishers'
Forum, which organises conferences and seminars
and the exchange of information and experiences.

Paul Hamlyn Foundation
18 Queen Anne's Gate, London SW1H 9AA
tel: 020 7227 3500
fax: 020 7222 0601
e-mail: information@phg.org.uk
Annual guide to skills training for publishers.
Offers grants to employees of small voluntary
organisations to improve publishing skills.

Essential reading

If you produce publications there are some
books you simply can't be without. These
include a first-class dictionary, a thesaurus,
an atlas, and:

* *Hart's Rules for Compositors and Readers*
(Oxford University Press,
ISBN 0-19-212983-X)

* *The Oxford Dictionary for Writers and Editors*
(Oxford University Press,
ISBN 0-19-212970-8)

* *The Cambridge Handbook of Copy-editing,*
by Judith Butcher (Cambridge University
Press, ISBN 0-52140074-0)

* *Fowler's Modern English Usage*
(Oxford University Press,
ISBN 0-19-869126-2)

Here are some other titles that will be valuable
additions to your bookshelf:

* *Type and Layout*, by Colin Wheildon
(Strathmoor Press, Berkeley, California 94710,
ISBN 0-9624891-5-8)

* *The* New *Designer's Handbook*,
by Alastair Campbell (Little, Brown &
Company, ISBN 0-316-90658-1)

* *The* New *Print Production Handbook,*
by David Bann (Little, Brown & Company,
ISBN 0-316-641510)

* *Ogilvy on Advertising*, by David Ogilvy
(Pan Books, London 1984)

* *Pictures on a Page*, by Harold Evans
(Heinemann, London 1982)

* *Asking Properly*, by George Smith
(The White Lion Press, London EC2Y 3AY,
ISBN 0-9518971-1-X)

* *Relationship Fundraising*, by Ken Burnett
(The White Lion Press, London EC2Y 3AY,
ISBN 0-9518971-0-1)

* *Friends for Life*, by Ken Burnett
(The White Lion Press, London EC2Y 3AY,
ISBN 0-9518971-2-8)

* *Clear Print Guidelines*, a fact sheet
by the RNIB, tel: 020 7388 1266

Acknowledgements

Thanks to all the organisations who have
generously allowed us to use examples of
their communications in this book.

Thanks also to all those people who gave
their help, views and advice:

Farida Anderson, Partners of Prisoners
    and Families Support Group
Baber Smith
Victor Basta, Broadview
Ruth Bender Atik, The Miscarriage
    Association
David Caines
David Carrington, PPP Healthcare
    Medical Trust
Charities Aid Foundation
The Chase
Rita Cole
Kim Cross, The Wellcome Trust
Sue Davidson, ActionAid
Tony Drakeford, London Wildlife Trust
Vicky Edwards
Pesh Framjee, Binder Hamlyn and
    Arthur Andersen
Paul Fredericks, The Charity Commission
Leris Harfield, Marks & Spencer plc
Chris Innes
Judith Ingham, Withers Solicitors
Emma James
Patrick Nash, TBF: the teacher
    support network
Jo Norton, The Prince's Trust
Kirsty Paterson, The Natural History
    Museum
Chris Russell
Nigel Semmens, British Council
Taylor McKenzie
Alec Trengrove, Bristows Solicitors
Patsy Westcott
Julian Wheatley
Philip Wilson, Sargent Cancer Care
    for Children
The Workroom

Glossary

Call-out
A short, three- or four-line excerpt from an article which is pulled out from the body copy to catch the reader's attention.

Cut-out
A photo where the subject has been cut out to remove the background.

Cropping
Using only a part of a photo, to focus in on the best bit and get rid of unwanted details (see page 84).

Drop cap
A large initial at the beginning of a section of text that drops into the lines of type below, used to draw the reader's eye to the start of the text (see page 96).

Drop shadow
A tint around an illustration, giving a 'shadow' or three-dimensional effect.

Duotone
A print with a two-colour half-tone made from a photograph which has been screened with a second colour.

Four-colour process
Printing which uses cyan (blue), magenta, yellow and black to produce a full-colour publication. This book uses four-colour process.

Half-tone
A photographic process which uses dots to allow you to reproduce the graduations of tone in a black and white photo.

ISDN
A fast means of sending artwork down the telephone from your designer's computer to the printing house.

Justified/unjustified
Justified type is where the lines are all the same length, to produce columns of text with straight sides. Unjustified type uses lines of text of different length, so that one side of the column (usually the right side) is 'ragged'. The text of this book is unjustified.

Leading
The space between lines of text.

Pantone
Mixing four colours to achieve the colour you want cannot always give consistent results. Use the Pantone Matching System (PMS) to specify a particular coloured ink.

Point size
A way of measuring the size of type.

Retouching
Correcting or improving a visual image.

Reverse out
Using white or light-coloured text on a solid or half-tone background.

Running head
A line of type which repeats, for example, a chapter heading at the top of a page or across a spread.

Second colour
In two-colour printing, the first colour is often black – the colour in which most of the type is printed. The second colour may be any colour you choose.

Serif/sans serif
Serif type has small terminating strokes on the individual letters. Generally used for large areas of text where legibility is vital. Sans serif (without serifs) text looks more contemporary, but is harder to read in large amounts so is usually used for headings and short blocks of text.

Special colour
When a Pantone colour (ie not cyan, magenta, black or yellow) is used in addition to a four-colour process, usually to add vibrancy or to ensure a consistent colour.

Subhead
A small heading used to break up dense columns of text, or to flag something up for the reader.

Tint
A shade of a colour produced by breaking up the colour into a formation of tiny dots. Also referred to as a percentage, where 10% is pale and 50% much stronger.

Tracking
The space between letters.

Typeface
A style of type – there are thousands to choose from. Also referred to as fonts.

White space
Don't be tempted to fill all the space on a page. White space can be used very effectively.

Final words

© Matt Cook

▲ An effective annual report is one which plants something so memorable, compelling and urgent in the reader's mind, that they just have to do something about it.

Annual reports matter, not because of how they look but because of what they represent and what they can do. We don't want people to pick up our annual reports and say 'what a great annual report'. We want readers to feel so well-informed, so stimulated, so reassured and refreshed in their commitment to the cause that they go out and tell their friends about us. We want readers to feel so motivated and inspired that they say, 'I must do something about this, and I must do it now'.

A good annual report is very much more than the minimum requirements of law and recommended practice. As we hope this book will have shown you, a good annual report should be firmly reader-led, the embodiment of your organisation's brand values, inspiring, beautiful, passionate, compelling, accessible, great value for money and the provoker of lots of varied, useful and valuable responses. And lots more besides.

So it follows that the act of producing such an annual report should itself be varied, challenging, stimulating, thrilling and rewarding, because that's what a good annual report has to be. Whatever your role in this fascinating and fulfilling process, we hope this book has helped you and will continue to help you in all your communications with the world outside your organisation.